T0328189

Cambridge Elements ≡

Elements in Law, Economics and Politics

Series Editor in Chief
Carmine Guerriero, *University of Bologna*

Series Co-Editors
Alessandro Riboni, *École Polytechnique*
Jillian Grennan, *Duke University, Fuqua School of Business*
Petros Sekeris, *Montpellier Business School*

A SAFETY VALVE MODEL OF EQUITY AS ANTI-OPPORTUNISM

Kenneth Ayotte
UC Berkeley School of Law

Ezra Friedman
Northwestern University Pritzker School of Law

Henry E. Smith
Harvard Law School

CAMBRIDGE
UNIVERSITY PRESS

CAMBRIDGE
UNIVERSITY PRESS

Shaftesbury Road, Cambridge CB2 8EA, United Kingdom

One Liberty Plaza, 20th Floor, New York, NY 10006, USA

477 Williamstown Road, Port Melbourne, VIC 3207, Australia

314–321, 3rd Floor, Plot 3, Splendor Forum, Jasola District Centre, New Delhi – 110025, India

103 Penang Road, #05–06/07, Visioncrest Commercial, Singapore 238467

Cambridge University Press is part of Cambridge University Press & Assessment, a department of the University of Cambridge.

We share the University's mission to contribute to society through the pursuit of education, learning and research at the highest international levels of excellence.

www.cambridge.org
Information on this title: www.cambridge.org/9781009217941

DOI: 10.1017/9781009217965

First published 2023

A catalogue record for this publication is available from the British Library.

ISBN 978-1-009-21794-1 Paperback
ISSN 2732-4931 (online)
ISSN 2732-4923 (print)

A Safety Valve Model of Equity as Anti-opportunism

Elements in Law, Economics and Politics

DOI: 10.1017/9781009217965
First published online: August 2023

The co-editor in charge of this submission was Carmine Guerriero.

Kenneth Ayotte
UC Berkeley School of Law

Ezra Friedman
Northwestern University Pritzker School of Law

Henry E. Smith
Harvard Law School

Author for correspondence: Kenneth Ayotte, kayotte@law.berkeley.edu

Abstract: Equity can be defined as the use of a more flexible, morally judgmental, and subjective mode of legal decision-making that roughly corresponds with historical equity. This Element presents a simple contracting model that captures the role of equity as a safety valve and shows how it can solve problems posed by opportunists – agents with an unusual willingness and ability to take advantage of necessary imperfections in the law. In this model, a simple but imperfect formal legal regime is able to achieve first-best in the absence of opportunists. But when opportunists are added, a more flexible regime (equity) can be preferred. However, equity is also vulnerable to being used opportunistically by the parties it intends to protect. Hence, the Element shows that it is often preferable to limit equity, reserving it for use only against those who appear sufficiently likely to be opportunists.

Keywords: equity, formalism, contextualism, opportunism, contracts

ISBNs: 9781009217941 (PB), 9781009217965 (OC)
ISSNs: 2732-4931 (online), 2732-4923 (print)

Contents

1   Introduction   1

2   Related Literature   4

3   Contracting Example   9

4   Comparative Statics   18

5   Further Applications   21

6   Discussion   25

7   Conclusion   36

    Appendix   38

    References   44

1 Introduction

That law is necessarily incomplete is an old truth whose implications have become clearer in the light of economic analysis. Putting pressure on the gaps in the law is the phenomenon of opportunism explored in depth by Oliver Williamson. In this Element, we resurrect another old notion related to the law's incompleteness – equity as a safety valve on the law – and show how it can be seen as part of the law's response to the problem of opportunism.

Both within law and economics, and more generally, responses to opportunism tend to paint with a broad brush. Formalists emphasize the need to be clearer about what constitutes bad behavior and to give effect to parties' directions to courts, while contextualists see the need for flexibility to respond to clever strategies for taking advantage of other actors. This debate is particularly stark in contract theory, where the question is whether parties are always in a better position than courts to anticipate and deal with the problem of opportunism, either through more detailed contractual provisions, through asset ownership, or through hierarchical organization.

These strands of the literature do not consider that it may be sensible to employ both formal and contextual approaches simultaneously and to structure and deploy these approaches selectively depending on the circumstances. Decision modes that go under the headings "law" and "equity"– especially prior to the merger of the separate courts of law and equity – provide an example of this approach. Equity, in the sense of equitable principles and remedies, modifies the applications of and supplements – "corrects" – the general, regular law when it has seriously gone off the rails, something one can term "meta-law" (Smith 2021). Among the problems of complexity and uncertainty that such intervention can address is opportunism, and equity provides a very general and venerable mechanism that is deployed selectively – as a "safety valve"– to deter opportunism (Smith 2011, 2017). We do not claim that discouraging opportunism is the exclusive justification for a contextual mode of decision-making or was the only function of equity. Nor do we argue that the law's efforts at countering opportunism were ever the exclusive province of equity. Instead, we model the safety valve function that was a major theme of equity and remains a major justification for departures from formalism.

Key to understanding the functional role that equity can (and often did) play is the need to discourage the types of opportunism emphasized in the work of Oliver Williamson. Williamson (1985, 47) defines opportunism as "self-interest seeking with guile." Equity traditionally focused on deception, often deceit that fell short of provable fraud. As earlier commentators realized, the problem with opportunism is that it is wealth-destroying but hard to foresee in its particulars, making it difficult to specify *ex ante*. On the other hand, reserving a large amount of discretion to define it *ex post* tends to chill behavior by innocent actors and to destabilize expectations that the law is supposed to foster. Essential to the distinction between opportunists and non-opportunists is an information asymmetry. In particular, the opportunist knows so much about the legal structure they face that they can take unintended and hard-to-foresee advantage of it.[1]

We present a simple contracting model that captures the role of equity as a safety valve to discourage opportunism. From a contract theory perspective, a novel aspect of our model is distinguishing opportunistic from non-opportunistic actors when all parties are self-interested. In our model, non-opportunistic buyers of a good (whom we call "garden-variety" buyers) have imperfect information about their rights under a contract after the good is delivered. Garden-variety actors observe the overall quality of the delivered good and thus have a credible threat to sue when overall quality is below contracted quality. But these actors must incur an investigation cost to match the precise characteristics of the delivered good to their entitlements under the contract. These investigation costs might arise *ex post* because garden-variety actors are "satisficing" actors who do not expect to litigate and hence do not invest in understanding and remembering the precise details of their contracts. If this investigation cost is high enough, technical breaches by sellers can go uncompensated. In our model, when technical breaches are not compensated, this can create beneficial welfare effects. They give sellers a greater incentive to make efficient, non-contractible substitutions in states of the world where technical compliance with the contract is inefficiently costly.

---

[1] More detailed contracts or legal rules are unlikely to be effective against such opportunism: As noted by Masten (1988, 182–183):

> While opportunism and moral hazard are similar in that both assume that actors look first to their own self interest, opportunism is more ingenious, active, and likely to provoke strategic responses by other parties than the type of noncooperative behavior assumed in agency models. Transactors are characterized by their cleverness, to the point of deviousness, in circumventing rules, discovering loopholes, or otherwise exploiting strategic advantages. Using contracts to try to induce cooperative behavior from an uncooperative actor is like trying to pick up mercury; every provision stipulated or contingency appended just creates another source of contention open to various interpretations and is thus subject to manipulation in court.

The flexibility and dynamism of opportunists require a flexible response of the sort embodied in equity.

We show, however, that a "substantive compliance" equilibrium between sellers and garden-variety buyers can be undermined by the presence of opportunist buyers. We see opportunists as distinct from garden-variety actors in the degree to which they are prone to take advantage of the incompleteness of the law. In our model, opportunists are agents who are fully aware of their legal entitlements and are willing to exploit them to their full advantage *ex post*. We model the difference between opportunist and garden-variety actors as one of legal sophistication, as opposed to morality, but our results would apply as well if all actors had equivalent knowledge but garden-variety actors were reluctant to exploit loopholes for moral or reputational reasons. In any case, even if a seller substantively complies with a contract by providing the agreed-upon quality, opportunists will sue on any technical breaches that occur. The damages paid by sellers to opportunist buyers introduce a transfer from garden-variety buyers to opportunist buyers in equilibrium, with two potential welfare costs. First, it may cause garden-variety types to contract for inefficiently lower quality to avoid subsidizing opportunists. Second, it might result in inefficient overconsumption by opportunists, even if garden-variety types continue to contract for high quality.

In this framework, an equitable intervention that allows sellers to avoid penalties by demonstrating substantive compliance can improve welfare. But the availability of this anti-opportunism device creates scope for a different type of opportunism by the sellers it seeks to protect. In particular, opportunist sellers might provide low quality and seek to avoid damages by invoking equity. We show that the costs of this kind of opportunism can be mitigated by using equity only as a "safety valve": equity should be applied by judges to protect sellers only when the judge is sufficiently certain that the buyer is an opportunist. We offer some intuitive comparative statics regarding the optimal expansiveness or restrictiveness of equity.

We believe these comparative statics are broadly consistent with casual observations of the use of equity in various areas of law. For example, our application of the model to patent law suggests that an increased likelihood that patent infringement claims are being brought by patent trolls should make courts more likely to refuse to issue injunctions and to simply assess monetary damages in close cases. Thus one might do time-series or panel studies across industries, comparing some measure of the prevalence of troll-like infringement with the likelihood of obtaining injunctive relief.[2]

---

[2] For descriptive results showing that patent assertion entities (loosely trolls) do not fare well in litigation, see Allison, Lemley, and Schwartz (2017). As we note in Section 6.2, how well the courts are targeting opportunists in this context is somewhat clouded by the US Supreme

Another area of law where casual empiricism is consistent with our theory is
the field of insurance, where legal doctrine has evolved in response to concerns
that insurers use formal rules opportunistically to deny coverage. Courts can
attempt to cabin such opportunistic formalism using doctrines such as *contra
proferentem*, which holds ambiguous provisions against the insurer/drafter to
prevent abuse of unclear contract terms. However, as described in the recently
promulgated *Restatement of the Law of Liability Insurance*,[3] courts limit use of
contra proferentem by suggesting it does not apply when the insured would not
reasonably expect coverage – that is to say that this equitable intervention is
not available when it appears to the court that it is being used opportunistically.

We will proceed as follows: Section 2 situates our work in relation to the
extant literature. In Section 3, we begin with a simple, stylized contracting
model between a buyer and a seller that illustrates the problem of opportunism.
We show that equitable intervention may be useful but only when applied as a
"safety valve" against those buyers that appear to be acting opportunistically. In
Section 4, we enrich the stylized model to generate some intuitive comparative
statics about the optimal degree of expansiveness of equity. Section 5 analyzes
patents and fraudulent transfers as potential applications of the model. Section 6
connects our work with insights from transaction cost economics. Section 7
concludes the Element.

2 Related Literature

Our model differs from the standard picture of *ex ante* contracting to bind
parties and thereby make possible mutually beneficial sets of actions. Some
elements of our safety valve model resonate with strains of the contracting
literature emphasizing vague standards, the role of opportunism, and fault in
contract law.

Vague standards have received attention from a well-developed literature
comparing the desirability of formal rules to flexible standards applied
to general legal questions. Works such as Ehrlich and Posner (1974) and
Kaplow (1992) have generally focused on the efficiency trade-off between
rules, which are easy to administer but inflexible, and standards, which require
skill and judgment to administer but can efficiently respond to factors that were
not contemplated *ex ante*. Vague standards can raise parties' costs and chill
legitimate behavior. Scott and Triantis (2006) argue that contractual parties

Court's opinion in *eBay* v. *MercExchange*, 547 U.S. 388 (2006). It is hard to tell how the Court's
opinion is operationalized, especially as to how disproportionate hardship works and whether
notions of good faith are in play (see Gergen et al. 2012).
[3] See *Restatement of the Law of Liability Insurance* §4(2) (2018).

make a similar trade-off when they incorporate vague terms in contracts, although Choi and Triantis (2008, 2010) show that the costs of using standards can serve to commit the parties and send effective signals by making *ex post* verification more costly. Friedman and Wickelgren (2014) look at how loose standards as opposed to formal rules may allow decision makers to respond to private information known only to the parties.

Carmine Guerriero (2020) constructs a model that suggests that when transaction costs are higher, or information asymmetry is greater, weaker property rights are socially desirable. In a cross-country analysis, he provides empirical evidence that suggests property rights tend to be weaker in the presence of higher transaction costs. Because weaker property rights tend to lead to more contextual and flexible resolution of legal disputes, we can see them as a form of equity, so these results are consistent with our prediction that more use of equity is desirable in the presence of increasing contractual incompleteness.

At the same time, there is a strand of contract theorizing that emphasizes the possibility of opportunism by contractual parties (see, e.g., Cohen 1992; Kostritsky 2007; Muris 1981). Opportunism is hard to define, but it is a cousin of fraud. The common theme in the opportunism literature is the ability of parties to misuse the contract and to commit deception that comes close to qualifying as fraud or is fraud that is too hard to prove under normal evidentiary presumptions (cf. Epstein 1975). This is actually a view that was prevalent in the nineteenth century and is close to the notion we employ in our analysis.[4] The opportunism literature is also open to the controversial notion of fault in contract law and is more oriented toward enforcement and sanctions than is mainstream law and economics (Cohen 2009). Not coincidentally, outside of law and economics, there is a deontological tradition in contract theory that likewise casts contractual behavior in terms of wrongs like promise-breaking and characterizes certain breaches as misappropriation requiring sanctions rather than prices (compare Friedmann [1989, 12] and Shiffrin [2007] with Kaplow and Shavell [2002, 172–213] and Shavell [2009]). Emblematic – but only emblematic – of some of these fissures in contract theory is the old debate over efficient breach. Although not all law and economics analysis points in the direction of efficient breach theory, the use of the language of fault and the

---

[4] On the nineteenth-century view that unconscionability referred to fraud that could not readily be proved, see, for example, *Seymour v. Delancey*, 3 Cow. 445, 521–522, 15 Am.Dec. 270 (N.Y. Sup. 1824) ("Inadequacy of price, unless it amount to conclusive evidence of fraud, is not itself a sufficient ground for refusing a specific performance of an agreement") (citing cases); Gordley (1981, 1587).

characterization of breach as a wrong that should not be priced are outside the mainstream of law and economics.

Related to notions of opportunism is the question of fault in contract law. Indeed, one method of dealing with opportunism is to define it as a wrong and to hold parties liable. In fact, acting opportunistically can be regarded as an egregious example of fault (willful rather than negligent). Or the response can be remedial, in which a pattern of behavior that one could label "willful" breach is used to get at undetectable bad behavior by "nasty" types, in a fashion reminiscent of theories of punitive damages based on the difficulty of detection (Bar-Gill & Ben-Shahar 2009). These works have generally focused on an *ex ante* choice of which modality would be applied to a particular class of cases or issues and do not suggest using different modalities for different litigants in similar situations, especially keyed to evasionary behavior itself. In contrast, our work is intended to serve as an explanation for why it might be desirable to modify the application of formal rules in scenarios where they might otherwise be efficient, based on the perception that a litigant is acting with guile, rather than ordinary self-interest.

Stremitzer (2012) considers a model in which buyers may be able to refuse delivery on the grounds of technical breach. Stremitzer's model finds that allowing (strategic or opportunistic) rejection for quasi-formalistic reasons can induce sellers to share rents in order to prevent inefficient cancellation of contracts. However, that paper is more focused on the distributional consequences of allowing inefficient remedies and is not aimed at exploring the interaction between equity and formalism, nor opportunism per se. As a result, the paper does not address when more flexible interpretations of contracts are superior.

In the following sections, we will develop a model of the equitable safety valve based on asymmetric information. In our model, all people are rational actors with varying amounts of information. Hence, for us, the problem in opportunism has much to do with levels and types of foreseeability. Opportunism of the sort we are interested in manifests in "loophole seeking" and the exploitation of "snags." The opportunist attempts to use the letter of the law to achieve objectives that are inconsistent with the law's purpose and in doing so creates net social costs (Smith 2021, 1050). In our model, some people (opportunists) have high levels of information about whether contractual performance (or by extension other relevant assets and activities) conform to the letter of the law even if they fully serve the law's purpose. The opportunists have an informational advantage over others (garden-variety) who holistically know that the purpose of the contract (or other law) has been served but find it too costly to find out whether the letter of the contract or law has been followed to a "T", or find it too costly to sue for the technical divergence. Because of the opportunist's superior information, it will be difficult and sometimes not cost-effective for contractual parties or policy makers *ex ante* to devise specific solutions aimed at specific forms of opportunism.

In Section 6, we return to the issue of deception and foreseeability in opportunistic behavior and argue that the problem is more dire and the solutions need to be more stringent, and more likely mandatory, if the opportunism is radically unforeseeable, in that the form it takes is a matter of (unquantifiable) uncertainty rather than (quantifiable) risk.

Our safety valve model of equity carries the potential to reconcile these strands of contract theory. Let us return to the definition of opportunism. The problem with some definitions of opportunism is that they are so broad that intervention would potentially be routine. For example, if we define opportunism as acting against the other party's expectations but within the letter of the contract (Muris 1981, 521), we still need to know how the expectation arose. Or, if opportunism is defined as acting "contrary to the parties' agreement, contractual norms, or conventional morality" (Cohen 2009, 1454), then it suffers from the breadth and indeterminacy of the open-ended appeal to moral intuition that irked the common law lawyers in their critique of equity. The opportunism literature has come under criticism for not paying attention to the parties' ability to choose methods of dealing with opportunism (see, e.g., Craswell 2009; Scott 2009, 2015). Particularly problematic are definitions that leave little scope for contracting parties to combat opportunism on their own. Thus, identifying opportunism with unfairness writ large or defining it as taking any advantage of the vulnerability of the other party, or as acting contrary to the other party's expectations, all point to a very wide notion of opportunism. Unfairness, vulnerability, and unilateral expectations allow courts to intervene in the ways that the new formalists find objectionable.

To return to Williamson's definition of self-interest seeking with guile (Williamson 1985, 47; 1993, 97), we need a definition of guile. Is all strategic behavior bad? Sometimes the law anticipates that people will shade the truth, and it reflects a judgment that it is common knowledge that one should not rely on certain representations literally. Thus, commercial "puffery," as where a car dealer says that no one is ever dissatisfied with a certain model, is not actionable fraud even if it is not true.[5] Likewise, the law often protects private information.

---

[5] It appears that the law does not categorically give priority to preventing opportunism over internalizing the effects of negligence (as argued by Cohen 1992); nor does it generally put the onus on the victim of deception not to be too vulnerable (Goldberg 1989, 71). Indeed, equity protects "ninnies" (Rose 1988, 588; Smith 2011) and "fools" (Pound, quoted by Cohen 1992), but as many have noticed in connection with doctrines like unconscionability, the focus is on

Thus, if someone does research and believes an asset is worth more than its market price, that person can buy the asset without revealing the information (see, e.g., Kronman 1978, 9–18). (The law has been ambivalent about people buying old masters at garage sales or oil-rich land from unsuspecting farmers. Protecting people from themselves and making them more willing to transact has to be balanced against their potential carelessness and the need for potential buyers to be able to appropriate the returns of developing information.) Perhaps the reason why Williamsonian guile and traditional notions of near-fraud suggest deception is that opportunism brings together two elements involved in classic deception: unexpectedness (on some level) and advantage-taking.

More promising is to define opportunism in the contractual setting as a special case of opportunism that gets past other devices for dealing with it. Opportunism in general appears to contain an element of deceit because the opportunist takes unanticipated or unintended advantage of the law to the detriment of others (and likely also social welfare), because the opportunism cannot be cost-effectively defined or prevented beforehand (Smith 2021, 1079.) In the contractual context, its unanticipated or unintended nature takes the behavior out of the shared contemplation of the parties but perhaps not out of the plans of the opportunist (if the opportunism is *ex ante*). In our model, the opportunist takes advantage of unusual knowledge about gaps in the contract or in the law. So, opportunism is using the law (or contract) in a way that it is not intended and can at most be anticipated in a general (and behavior-distorting) sense. The understanding that counterparties will sometimes use the imprecision to their advantage reduces the seller's incentive to act efficiently.

Our focus in this Element is on the optimal contours of equity: why it should be applied against opportunistic actors in particular, why it should be applied only sparingly, and when it should be more or less expansive. As such, we do not offer a new explanation for why equity should be mandatory. Mandatory rules have been justified on grounds such as eliminating socially wasteful signaling (Aghion & Hermalin 1990) and bounded rationality. Likewise, asymmetric information about types can inhibit socially efficient investments in completing contracts (Spier 1992). A further argument in favor of mandatory rules in the context of opportunism is that choices of contract terms can make exploitation of the naive more profitable (Friedman 2013). Those who distrust these explanations can read our analysis more conservatively as providing the contours of optimal default rules, from which sophisticated parties may be allowed to opt out.

---

the conduct of the scoundrel or opportunist. Cohen (1992, 971); Epstein (1975); Rose (1988); Smith (2011).

3 Contracting Example

Imagine that buyers contract to purchase goods from a marketplace of competitive sellers. Buyers value quality (x), which the seller can provide through components a or b, so that $x = a + b$. We suppose that contracts are incomplete, in that they can describe a with precision but they cannot specify b or x. For the sake of concreteness, the seller might be a builder and the buyer a homeowner. The homeowner might be able to specify a characteristic of the house that they value (granite countertops from a particular manufacturer, which represents $a = 1$) but might not be able to describe all potential substitutes (this would represent $b = 1$) that would be equally desirable.

We assume that quality $x = 1$ is always efficient but that the efficient way of obtaining $x = 1$ depends on a non-contractible state of the world that is unobservable *ex ante*. With probability $1 - \pi$, the usual state obtains, and the cheapest way of achieving $x = 1$ is by setting $a = 1$. In this case, the cost of setting $a = 1$ is z_L. But with probability π, the unusual state obtains, and the cheapest way of obtaining $x = 1$ is with $b = 1$, again at a cost of z_L. We assume that neither the buyer nor the court can directly observe whether the usual or unusual state obtains. Because a can be specified in a contract but b cannot, the probability of the unusual state π is a measure of the degree of contractual incompleteness.

In both states, we assume that the cost of achieving high quality in the less efficient way is $z_H > z_L$. In the context of our homeowner/builder example, this captures the possibility that in some states of the world, full compliance with the explicit terms of a contract may be costly. Supplies of the particular granite may be temporarily unavailable to the builder, and the use of a close substitute countertop may be required. Since little is lost by doing so, we will simplify the model by assuming that $z_H = \infty$, implying that technical compliance with the letter of the contract in all states of the world is impossible.[6] Consider an example where values are given as in Table 1.

The state contingent costs are as given in Table 2. Assume that the seller can always supply the good with $a = 0$ and $b = 0$ at a cost of 0. Our assumption that quality $x = 1$ is always efficient implies that $V_1 > z_L$.

Formally, the timing of the game is as follows: In period 0, sellers offer contracts and buyers choose whether to purchase the good. In period 1, the state is revealed to sellers and sellers decide whether and how to invest in quality. In

---

[6] In an earlier version of the model, we consider a finite z_H. This gives the garden-variety seller an additional option when opportunists enter the market: The seller can choose to technically comply with the contract by providing $a = 1$ in the unusual state. Adding this option limits the costs of opportunism to the extent that z_H is not too large.

Table 1 Value
to buyer

x	V
1	V_1
0	0

Table 2 Costs of investments

State	Probability	Cost for $a = 0$ & $b = 0$	Cost for $a = 1$	Cost for $b = 1$
Usual	$1 - \pi$	0	z_L	$z_H = \infty$
Unusual	π	0	$z_H = \infty$	z_L

period 2, the buyers receive the good and make a decision on whether or not to sue for breach. In period 3, the court decides whether to find breach and how much damages to assess.

3.1 Garden-Variety Buyers

We assume that garden-variety buyers are limited in their ability or desire to exploit their contractual rights in full. They might, for example, have cognitive limitations that prevent them from remembering the full details of the contract or limitations that prevent them from discovering the precise characteristics of the good they receive from the seller. Hence, it is not always obvious to them whether there was a technical breach or not.

Concretely, we suppose that garden-variety buyers observe the total quality x, so they know whether they are satisfied with the final outcome, but they must incur a cost of c to investigate the seller's means of compliance and observe a or b. If they are dissatisfied, they may infer that a breach is likely to have occurred but they are not able to sue without paying a cost of c to uncover evidence of the breach.

For expositional purposes, we will say that the seller provides *substantive compliance* when high-quality goods are provided in both states ($a = 1$ in the usual state and $b = 1$ in the unusual state), *partial compliance* when high quality is provided only in the usual state ($a = 1$ in the usual state and $x = 0$ in the unusual state), and *low quality* when $x = 0$ in both states.

Remark 1. *In this setting, a first-best allocation requires that the seller provide substantive compliance and no investigation costs are incurred by buyers.*

In Lemma 1, we show that if c is not too low, the first-best can be sustained by contracting on only the verifiable component of quality (a):

Lemma 1. *If all buyers are garden-variety and $c \geq \pi z_L$, an optimal contract requires that the seller provide $a = 1$. The buyer agrees to pay a price $P = z_L$ and can recover damages $D \in (\max(z_L, c), \frac{c}{\pi})$ if the seller breaches. This optimal contract implements the first-best allocation.*

If $c < \pi z_L$, substantive compliance will not be provided by sellers in any equilibrium.

Proof. Since $D \geq c$, the buyer will find it incentive-compatible to investigate if high quality is not provided, and since $c \geq \max(\pi z_L, \pi c)$, it is incentive-compatible for the buyer to not sue when high quality is provided. The buyer will win any suit where high quality is not provided (since $a = 1$ was promised and not delivered). Since $D \geq z_L$, the seller prefers to provide high quality to breaching in both states. The price $P = z_L$ is sufficient to satisfy the seller's participation constraint and gives the buyer a surplus $V_1 - z_L > 0$.

If $c < \pi z_L$, then any $D \geq z_L$ that gives the seller incentive to provide $a = 1$ in the unusual state rather than breach also gives the buyer incentive to investigate, even if high quality is received. The buyer's suit would be successful in the unusual state, so the buyer would receive an expected payment of $\pi D \geq \pi z_L > c$. Given that providing $b = 1$ in the unusual state does not deter a suit, the seller has no incentive to provide it. ∎

In effect, the buyer's ignorance can increase the efficiency of the contract. The buyer's lack of knowledge about the precise details of the contract gives the seller an incentive to make efficient but non-contractible substitutions when these substitutions deter lawsuits.

3.2 Opportunists

Now imagine that a proportion q of the buyers are opportunists. Opportunists in our model are actors who have full knowledge of the contract and the characteristics of the goods they receive. Concretely, we suppose they observe a and b at no cost. Hence, opportunists are fully aware of their legal entitlements and willing to exploit them. If they write a contract that promises $a = 1$, opportunists will sue whenever $a = 0$ if the damages justify the cost of suit, irrespective of whether the seller provides $b = 1$. In our model, opportunists are no more self-interested than others; they simply have a technical advantage in exploiting the fine points of a contract. However our results would apply just as well if garden-variety buyers faced constraints such as norms, morals, or reputational concerns that did not constrain opportunists. The important feature of opportunists in our model is that they are particularly prone to exploit loopholes or weaknesses in formal law.

We assume that sellers know the proportion of buyers who are opportunist but cannot tell the difference between opportunist and garden-variety buyers.[7] The addition of unobservable opportunists changes the contracting game between garden-variety buyers and sellers, making a substantive compliance equilibrium more difficult to sustain. In the unusual state, the seller expects to be sued by opportunists regardless of whether or not they provide $b = 1$. Because sellers now expect that substantive compliance avoids a lawsuit with only probability $1 - q$, sellers must be given a greater incentive to provide non-contractible quality by raising D. Specifically, sellers now provide $b = 1$ in the unusual state only if $D \geq \frac{z_L}{1-q}$. Second, the sellers now expect higher costs, which they must pass on to buyers. Rather than expecting a cost of z_L, the seller expects to spend an extra $q\pi D$ to cover the expected cost of damages from lawsuits by opportunists in the unusual state. Thus, the minimum expected cost of purchasing the good for the garden-variety buyer rises to $z_L + q\pi D$.

The next proposition shows that opportunists make a substantive compliance equilibrium harder to sustain. Further, any substantive compliance equilibrium involves a cross-subsidy from garden-variety buyers to opportunists:

Proposition 2. *For any* $q \geq \min\{\frac{c-\pi z_L}{c}, \frac{V_1-z_L+c}{V_1+c}, \frac{V_1-z_L}{V_1-(1-\pi)z_L}\}$, *substantive compliance will not be provided in any equilibrium. When there is a positive proportion of opportunists* $(q > 0)$, *any substantive compliance equilibrium requires a cross-subsidy from garden-variety to opportunist buyers.*

Proof. The following are necessary conditions for substantive compliance to be provided in equilibrium:

(a) D must be set so that garden-variety buyers do not sue if they receive high quality, otherwise sellers will not provide $b = 1$ in the unusual state. This requires $D \leq \frac{c}{\pi}$.

(b) Providing $b = 1$ in the unusual state is incentive-compatible for the seller. This requires $D \geq \frac{z_L}{1-q}$.

(c) The seller's participation constraint is satisfied. This requires that $P \geq z_L + q\pi D$.

(d) Garden-variety buyers prefer a substantive compliance contract to a partial compliance equilibrium. Under partial compliance, the seller provides the

---

[7] We view this as consistent with a notion that traders are aware of the presence of opportunism in general but may not be aware of how exactly opportunists are likely to operate.

quality good in the usual state, but in the unusual state the seller provides low quality and is sued by all buyers. Thus, the cost to sellers of providing partial compliance is $(1 - \pi)z_L + \pi D$. Under partial compliance, garden-variety buyers receive a quality good in the usual state, and in the unusual state they pay cost c to uncover the breach and receive damages D. Since sellers price to cover their costs, the surplus from the partial compliance is $(1-\pi)(V_1)+\pi D-\pi c-((1-\pi)z_L+\pi D)$. Thus, full compliance is preferable because $V_1 - P \geq (1 - \pi)V_1 + \pi(z_L - c) - z_L$.

(e) Garden-variety buyers prefer a substantive compliance contract to a low-quality contract. This requires $V_1 - P \geq 0$.

For (a) and (b) to hold simultaneously, $q \leq \frac{c-\pi z_L}{c}$. For conditions (b),(c), and (d) to hold, $q \leq \frac{V_1-z_L+c}{V_1+c}$. And for (b),(c), and (e) to hold, $q \leq \frac{V_1-z_L}{\pi z_L+(V_1-z_L)}$.

To establish the second part of the proposition, note that since the market for sellers is competitive, the seller's participation constraint always binds, so $P = z_L + q\pi D$ in a substantive compliance equilibrium. Thus, garden-variety buyers pay more than the cost of the good (z_L) and receive no damages. Since opportunists receive expected damages πD, they pay an effective price $P' = P - \pi D = z_L - (1 - q)\pi D < z_L$. ∎

The presence of opportunists creates problems from a social welfare perspective. In particular, if there are too many opportunists, there will be no market equilibrium where sellers always provide the efficient level of quality. Garden-variety types subsidize opportunists because they bear part of the expected cost of the damage payments through the price of the good. If this transfer becomes too large, garden-variety purchasers will eliminate the cross-subsidy to opportunists by contracting for lower quality.

This cross-subsidy can be eliminated in one of two ways. One way is for garden-variety buyers to offer sellers a "partial compliance" contract that sets $D = \max(z_L, c)$, so that sellers will have incentive to provide high quality only in the usual state. In the unusual state, sellers will provide low quality, and all buyers will sue. The buyer will offer the seller a price $P = (1 - \pi)z_L + \pi \max(z_L, c)$, at which the seller expects to break even. As described in the proof, net of the price, the value of the partial compliance contract to the garden-variety buyer will be

$$(1 - \pi)(V_1 - z_L) - \pi c.$$

Alternatively, the buyer can contract for a low-quality good, which costs 0 and has a value of 0 to the buyer. The garden-variety buyer prefers the partial compliance contract to the low-quality contract if and only if the expected surplus in the usual state outweighs the deadweight investigation costs in the unusual state: $(1 - \pi)(V_1 - z_L) > \pi c$.

In this simple setup, the transfer from garden-variety buyers to opportunists has welfare costs only if it causes the garden-variety buyers to contract for lower quality. In section 4, we explore a richer model with an additional cost: If there is any elasticity in the purchasing decision of either the garden-variety or opportunist buyers, this transfer will cause them to inefficiently distort their purchasing decisions. Because the garden-variety buyers are subsidizing the opportunists, they might not purchase in a competitive market, even when the value they place on the good is greater than the cost of producing it. Likewise, opportunist buyers receive this transfer when they purchase the good and might decide to purchase when the production cost is greater than the value of the good to them.

3.3 Equity

If courts could perfectly observe quality, they could easily solve the problem of opportunist buyers by applying equity and refusing to enforce damages for breach whenever it observes substantive compliance by the seller. This would ensure that sellers always had an incentive to provide quality and there would be no room for opportunists to game the contract.

In this section, we consider a cost to equitable intervention: When applied imperfectly by courts, equitable intervention that deters opportunism on one side of the transaction can increase the scope for opportunism on the other side. We show that, in response, it may be optimal for equity to be used only as a safety valve. In other words, it may be optimal to apply the equitable defense only when the court has sufficient confidence that the buyer is acting opportunistically. Thus, unlike a defense of substantive compliance, the availability of equity does not depend solely on the court's estimation of the magnitude of the performance shortfall but also depends on an evaluation of the intention of the parties.[8] To see this, we introduce the presence of opportunist sellers and imperfect courts. We imagine that courts can observe a potentially manipulable signal of substantive performance, denoted y. Specifically, we will assume that $y = x + f$, where f is a confounding signal that can be produced by opportunist sellers. We assume that y is not contractible, because quality cannot be precisely defined beforehand and all acceptable methods of substitution cannot be anticipated. The court forms an opinion about the quality of the

---

[8] For an explanation of the interplay between the defense of the right of rejection, substantive compliance, and incentives to perform in the presence of under compensation by the courts see Ganglmair (2017).

seller's performance at the time of lawsuit. We argue that basing the legal outcome on y requires equitable powers, because it requires the court to base its decision on factors that are not specified in the contract.

Definition 1. *A court applies equity when it refuses remedies for breach upon observing $y = 1$.*

Opportunist sellers can provide only "fake" substantive compliance by choosing an action $f = 1$ at a cost $z_O < z_L$. We assume that the other "honest" sellers are unable to produce $f = 1$. One can think of these opportunist sellers as parties who are experts at appearing sympathetic to the court or alternatively as parties that are simply favored by the court *ex ante*.[9] To gain some intuition, we start by assuming an infinitely elastic supply of opportunist sellers. Opportunists will enter the market whenever it is profitable to do so, and they exist in a supply that is large relative to honest sellers. In the simulation, we consider a scenario where there is elasticity in the supply of opportunistic sellers, and they represent a soft constraint on the use of equity to protect innocent sellers. We obtain qualitatively similar results.

3.3.1 Expansive Use of Equity and Market Breakdown

Because the court observes y but not b or x or f, an opportunistic seller can convince a judge who is applying equity that there was substantive compliance. Suppose, first, that the equity defense were available whenever the court observes substantive compliance, irrespective of the buyer's perceived type. The advantage of a broad application of equity is that it provides more protection to honest sellers. All opportunistic lawsuits by buyers will be deterred (opportunist buyers who appear to be garden-variety buyers can never collect damages), so honest sellers can break even by charging their marginal cost z_L. But courts cannot distinguish substantive from fake compliance. The next lemma shows that an overly expansive use of equity, just like the absence of equity, can cause a substantive compliance equilibrium to break down:

Lemma 3. *Suppose that courts always apply the equity defense whenever they observe substantive compliance by sellers. Then, the only equilibrium is a low-quality equilibrium.*

---

[9] To keep things simple, we assume here that courts are completely unable to distinguish opportunist from honest sellers. To the extent that separation is possible, it will always be efficient to deny the equitable remedy to opportunist sellers. Doing so would deter the entry of opportunist sellers without creating the undesirable transfer from garden-variety buyers to opportunistic buyers. One can think of this as the idea that those who seek equity must come with "clean hands."

Proof. Suppose there is an equilibrium where honest sellers provide high-quality goods. In any such equilibrium, a contract must provide that when $a = 1$ is provided, buyers will pay some price P equal to at least the honest seller's cost z_L. Damages D must also be at least z_L to prevent the honest seller from breaching. The equitable defense allows sellers to also receive P and pay no damages whenever the contract calls for $a = 1$ and the seller provides substantive compliance ($b = 1$ for the honest seller). Hence, honest sellers will provide $b = 1$ in the unusual state for any contract that induces high quality ($a = 1$) in the usual state.

But if an honest seller charges $P \geq z_L$, then the best response of opportunist sellers is to enter the market, offer the same contractual terms (P, D) that honest sellers offer, and provide $f = 1$ in both states. These sellers will earn a profit of $P - z_O \geq z_L - z_O > 0$. But since the supply of opportunist sellers is presumed to be large relative to honest sellers, and $f = 1$ is worthless to buyers, no buyer will pay a positive price for this contract: They will receive a good with no value and have no ability to collect damages. ∎

In this more simplified setup, opportunist sellers cause the market to break down entirely when they enter. This follows from our strong assumption that there is a large, elastic supply of opportunist sellers, an assumption we relax in in section 4. More generally, though, the lemma illustrates that applying equity too broadly can create too much incentive for opportunist sellers to enter the market, and this causes garden-variety buyers to shy away from contracting for quality.

3.3.2 Equity as a Safety Valve

One potential response to this problem is for the courts to only use equity against those whom the courts have a reason to believe are acting opportunistically. Here, we suppose that the courts receive an imperfect signal $S \in \{g, o\}$ about whether the plaintiff buyer is a garden-variety buyer or an opportunist. When the plaintiff is an opportunist, the court receives the correct signal (o) with probability $s > .5$. When the plaintiff is garden-variety, the court receives the correct signal g with probability s.

Suppose, now, that equitable relief for the seller is only available if the court receives the signal that the buyer is an opportunist. If an honest seller anticipates providing substantive compliance in the unusual state, she must now charge a price $P \geq z_L + D\pi q(1 - s)$ to break even. The premium $D\pi q(1 - s)$ is required to cover the costs of damages paid to opportunist buyers when substantive compliance is provided, but the court fails to recognize the buyer as an opportunist.

Now consider the entry decision of opportunist sellers. To break even, these sellers must charge at least $z_O + D((1-q)s + q(1-s))$. All buyers sue opportunist sellers, and damages are paid in the event that the buyer appears garden-variety to the court. For these sellers to be deterred from entry, it must be the case that their costs, inclusive of damages, exceed the price charged by honest sellers. This requires

$$z_O + D((1-q)s + q(1-s)) \geq z_L + D\pi q(1-s),$$

or

$$D \geq \frac{z_L - z_O}{(1-q)s + (1-\pi)q(1-s)}. \tag{1}$$

The opportunist seller pays damages in two circumstances that the honest seller does not. First, opportunist sellers pay damages whenever they supply a garden-variety buyer who is properly identified by the court: this happens with probability $(1-q)s$. Garden-variety buyers do not sue honest sellers who provide substantive compliance. Second, opportunist sellers pay damages in the usual state when the opportunist buyer is misidentified as garden-variety.[10] This occurs with probability $(1-\pi)q(1-s)$. Honest sellers provide actual compliance in the usual state, so opportunist buyers do not sue in that event. Insistence on formal interpretation under some circumstances protects against two-sided opportunism. As long as D is set high enough, the ability to impose greater expected damages on opportunist than honest sellers can keep opportunists out of the market. Recall, though, that the cross-subsidy from garden-variety buyers to opportunist buyers rises in D; hence, D cannot be so large that the garden-variety buyers opt out and contract for low quality instead. We formalize this in the next proposition:

Proposition 4. *Suppose courts allow an equitable defense only as a "safety valve": it is applied in favor of sellers if and only if the buyer appears to be an opportunist (if $S = o$). If $\frac{z_L - z_O}{(1-q)s + (1-\pi)q(1-s)} < \frac{V_1 - z_L}{\pi q(1-s)}$, there is a substantive compliance equilibrium in which opportunist sellers do not enter the market.*

Proof. For the garden-variety buyer to prefer the substantive compliance equilibrium to a low quality equilibrium requires that $V_1 - z_L - D\pi q(1-s) \geq 0$. Combining this inequality with the condition that deters entry by opportunists, (1), produces the inequality in the proposition. ∎

---

[10] With these assumptions, it is possible that even if $s < 0.5$, it might be possible to deter these sellers, although welfare is increasing in s.

4 Comparative Statics

The section above considers two possibilities for using the opportunism signal S: The court either ignores it or relies on it entirely to determine whether the equitable defense to damages is available to the seller. In general, neither approach is an optimal use of the signal. If entry by opportunistic sellers is not much of a threat, it may be optimal to use equity more expansively, by applying it with positive probability against seemingly garden-variety buyers. Because courts make errors, more aggressive use of equity can sweep in more opportunist buyers without encouraging opportunist sellers to enter, and this is welfare-enhancing. Conversely, if too many opportunistic sellers prefer to enter the market when the equity defense is valid only against seemingly opportunist buyers, the opportunist sellers might be further discouraged by a more restrictive use of equity. The equity defense could be applied with probability less than one when the judge perceives the buyer to be an opportunist.

This leads to a natural question: When should equity be more restrictive or expansive? In the Appendix, we develop a simulation of a market with elastic demand and both types of buyers, and we examine how the equilibrium in the market depends on the characteristics of the participants and the extent of the use of equity.

In order to consider the intuition that more expansive use of equity against buyers is likely to lead to more opportunist sellers, we now assume that the elasticity of opportunist sellers is finite. We introduce the parameter θ to represent the elasticity of opportunist sellers. Likewise, in order to measure the extent of welfare loss due to cross subsidization between buyers, we use ϕ as a parameter for the elasticity of buyers. Very briefly, the simulation finds a market equilibrium where honest sellers set prices at the competitive level given the equilibrium level of purchases by opportunist and garden-variety buyers. Finding an equilibrium is a matter of numerically solving four equations that consist of equation (1) a zero profit condition for innocent sellers and equations (2)–(4) that describe the indifference conditions for the marginal opportunist buyer, marginal garden-variety buyer, and marginal opportunist seller respectively. We then subject the equilibrium to the incentive compatibility constraint that ensures a substantive compliance equilibrium. A detailed description of the simulation is provided in the Appendix.

Specifically, we are interested in how the optimal extent of equity varies according to various parameters in the simulation. To be more concrete, we define τ_o as the likelihood that equity is applied when the court receives a signal that the buyer is opportunist and conjecture as follows:

Conjecture 5. *Our conjecture is that more use of equity against apparent opportunists will be optimal, so τ_O will be higher, when:*

(a) Contracts are less complete, so the probability of the unusual state, π, is higher;

(b) The accuracy of the court's signal of buyer opportunism, s, is higher;

(c) The proportion of opportunists among potential buyers, q, is higher;

(d) The proportion of opportunist sellers, θ, is lower; or

(e) The elasticity of buyers, ϕ, is higher.

Figures 1–5 illustrate the results of our simulations, which offer support for our conjectures. Each figure shows how the optimal expansiveness of equity varies as one parameter is varied, holding all other parameters constant.[11]

Figure 1 illustrates part (a), showing that the optimal intensity of equity is greater when the degree of contractual incompleteness is greater (i.e., when the unusual state is more likely). The intuition is that when π is higher, the need for equity is greater, because it is more likely that the parties will find themselves in a situation that they could not have efficiently contracted for *ex ante*. Because contracts are more incomplete, the scope for opportunistic lawsuits and the potential transfer to opportunists are greater, and it is more important to guard against these transfers with the use of equity.

Figure 2 illustrates part (b), showing the optimal intensity of equity increasing when the accuracy of the court's signal improves. When the court is able to accurately identify opportunist buyers, it can be more confident its use of equity is decreasing buyer opportunism without unduly encouraging

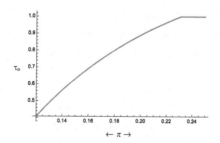

Figure 1 Optimal τ_O vs. π

[11] In each of these graphs, the values of the parameters that are not being varied are held to the default values given by $\{D = 50, \phi = 1, \theta = 0.4, s = 0.7, z_L = 20, V_1 = 50, \pi = 0.15, q = 0.2, z_O = -30, \bar{v} = 0\}$.

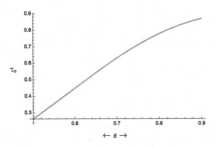

Figure 2 Optimal τ_0 vs. s

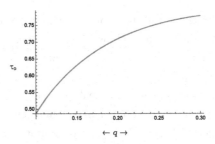

Figure 3 Optimal τ_0 vs. q

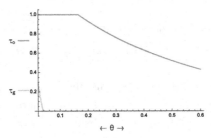

Figure 4 Optimal τ_0 and τ_g vs. θ

opportunist sellers to enter. Put differently, it is less likely that its use of equity is frustrating a plaintiff with a legitimate complaint in its effort to protect honest sellers.

Figure 3 illustrates that increasing the proportion of opportunist buyers increases the optimal use of equity, as suggested in part (c). When there are more opportunist buyers, the transfers enabled by not using equity are greater. Furthermore, the transfers to opportunist buyers are spread over fewer garden-variety buyers, so they create more harmful distortion in the form of underconsumption of the good by garden-variety buyers.

Figure 4 illustrates part (d) of the conjecture and shows the optimal intensity of equity decreasing as the number of potential opportunist sellers increases.

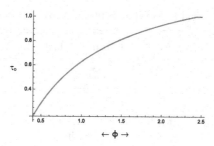

Figure 5 Optimal τ_0 vs. ϕ

This occurs because it is more costly to use equity when there are more opportunist sellers who will attempt to use it inappropriately. The flat portion at the left side of the graph of τ_o occurs where $\tau_o = 1$. At that point, any increase in the use of equity must be accomplished by raising τ_g when the court has received a signal that the plaintiff is garden-variety. Because applying equity under these circumstances is much less effective in reducing the cross-subsidy, it is not optimal to do so unless there are very few opportunist sellers, as seen by the fact that optimal $\tau_g > 0$ only when θ is very low. In all the other figures in this section, optimal τ_g is zero for all parameters and is not shown.

Finally, part (e) is illustrated in Figure 5. When the demand of buyers is very elastic, the consequences of the distortion created by the transfer from garden-variety types to opportunists is more severe, so it is more important to prevent it.

5 Further Applications

We have focused on the role of equity as a safety valve preventing opportunistic use of the law in contractual situations. However, our results would apply similarly to the use of equity in other legal situations. In this section, we discuss how our model might be applied to intellectual property and the problem of fraudulent transfer in bankruptcy.

5.1 Patents

Here, we present an example to consider how equity can be useful to prevent opportunistic patent use. Imagine that instead of a buyer and a seller we have an entrant and an incumbent. The incumbent has a patent, and society wants to reward the incumbent patent holder by preventing any copying of the invention that diminishes the value of the invention to the patent holder by competing with the patent.

Imagine that with probability $1 - \pi$ there is a typical entrant, who has three possible strategies. The entrant can (*A*) intentionally copy the product, (*B*)

Table 3 Typical entrant's profits

Profit from A	Profit from B	Profit from C
Y_H	Y_L	$Y_L - \eta$

Table 4 Social value of
incumbent's profits

Entrant's action	V
A	0
B	0
C	V_H

attempt to develop a "me-too" product that is inspired by the incumbent's product and competes with it but does not violate the incumbent's intellectual property rights, or (*C*) attempt to develop a noncompetitive product that does not affect the incumbent's profits. We assume that if the entrant chooses *A* the patent is always infringed. If the entrant chooses *B* or *C* the patent is infringed with likelihood λ. We assume that the typical entrant's profits are as given in Table 3.

We assume that with probability π there is an atypical entrant. This type of entrant cannot choose *B* or *C*; they can only engage in *A* at a profit of $Y_A \gg Max(Y_H, V_H)$. Note that this implies that when the incumbent observes copying (because the entrant has chosen either *A* or *B*), the likelihood of infringement is at least $\pi + (1-\pi)\lambda$. We note that in order to dissuade entrants from intentionally copying, damages, *D*, must be set at at least $Y_H - (Y_L - \eta)$.

A generally accepted goal of the patent system is encouraging innovation, and we assume for purposes of argument here that it is doing more good than harm in this respect. Thus, we assume then that there is social value to protecting the incumbent's profits from its patented products, as given in Table 4. Note that with a typical entrant our assumptions imply it is socially efficient for the entrant to take action *C* and develop a new product. However, the infringement is so profitable for the atypical entrant that it is actually socially efficient to copy (action *A*). It is never socially efficient for any entrant to develop the "me-too" product.

Again, we define one type of incumbent as "garden-variety." These incumbents can observe whether or not the entrant's product is a competitive product or a noncompetitive product, but they would need to pay a cost *c* to observe whether the product actually infringes on the patent. If no typical entrants intentionally copy, as long as $D < \frac{c}{\lambda}$, a garden-variety incumbent will not wish to investigate when the product does not compete. If $D > \frac{c}{\pi + (1-\pi)\lambda}$, a garden-variety entrant will investigate and sue when the product competes. When the incumbent sues if and only if the new product competes, then as long as $D > \frac{\eta}{\lambda}$, the entrant would prefer to market the new product that does not compete rather than the me-too product that does compete. So if $c > \eta$ and D is set so $\frac{c}{p_0 + (1-p_0)\lambda} < D < \frac{c}{\lambda}$, we will have an equilibrium where the incumbent will only sue if there is a product that competes. Because avoiding the me-too product is likely to prevent a lawsuit, even though it does not affect the likelihood of technical infringement, the entrant has incentive to avoid me-too products.

Now imagine a substantial fraction (q) of incumbents are opportunists (or patent trolls) and can observe any technical infringement, regardless of whether the new product competes with the incumbents.[12] Because avoiding the me-too product does not discourage lawsuits by opportunists, the presence of opportunists diminishes the incentive to avoid the me-too product. The difference in legal costs that the entrant faces when choosing between strategies B and C is now $(1 - q)\lambda D$ and the damages must be increased to at least $\frac{\eta}{\lambda(1-q)}$ for C to be preferable. Note that the legal costs from C are $q\lambda D$, so if $q\lambda D > \pi_L - \eta$, the entrant will not wish to produce anything. As the proportion of opportunists increases, damages increase further and the good equilibrium might be destroyed. Either $c < \frac{\eta}{1-q}$, so garden-variety types will always sue and innovators have no incentive to avoid the me-too product, or $q\frac{\eta}{\lambda(1-q)} > \pi_L - \eta$, so that the costs of lawsuits based on technical infringements are so large that the entrant does not bother innovating.

The intuition behind this example is very similar to the contracting example. In both cases, garden-variety actors' best indication of when they have a strong case is when they observe the antisocial behavior the law is trying to discourage. Consequently, the other parties have an incentive to avoid antisocial behavior even when it does not correspond exactly with the law. On the other hand, because of the opportunists' superior knowledge of the law, a party faced with an opportunist will know that avoiding the antisocial behavior may not help them at all, and they will thus be more tempted by the antisocial behavior.

---

[12] An alternative assumption that would lead to the same results but might be a better fit for technology industries is that garden-variety types suffer a cost c when they sue an entrant with a noncompetitive product, because they might invite a patent suit in retribution, but that opportunists (trolls) do not suffer these costs because they do not directly participate in the market.

5.2 Fraudulent Transfer

Fraudulent transfer is another example that illustrates some of the trade-offs behind our model. Fraudulent transfer statutes target transfers between a financially distressed debtor and a third party that have the effect of diverting value from creditors. Insolvent corporate debtors can act opportunistically to evade creditor claims in a variety of ways. In a business context, a corporation might pay a large dividend to shareholders in the wake of default. Within a corporate group, an insolvent subsidiary might sell assets at a below-market rate to a healthy one. A parent might borrow money and use a subsidiary to provide a guarantee. Once identified as a fraudulent transfer, the bankruptcy trustee can avoid the transaction and recover the lost value for the benefit of creditors.

The Bankruptcy Code[13] (and state fraudulent transfer laws, which can be used by the trustee in bankruptcy) attempt to isolate those transactions that arise from debtor opportunism. In particular, one way a trustee can avoid a transaction is to demonstrate intent by the debtor to "hinder, delay or defraud" a creditor.[14] Typical "badges of fraud" used to demonstrate intent include concealed transactions, transfers to insiders, and absconding by the debtor after the transfer.[15] Alternatively, the trustee can avoid a transfer as substantively fraudulent by showing that the debtor did not receive "reasonably equivalent value" for the transfer and the debtor was in a financially shaky position when the transfer was made.[16] Though an objective test, the two-prong test for constructive fraud also targets opportunistic transactions, as it is unlikely to be in a debtor's interest to transfer assets and receive less than full value in return.

In addition to targeting the law to opportunistic transactions, remedies also vary depending on the perceived opportunism of the parties. The recipient of a fraudulent transfer who acts in good faith is generally restored to their position before the transaction took place, by receiving a lien against the debtor to the extent of the value given. A third-party recipient who acts in bad faith is not entitled to a lien.[17]

Our model highlights the difficult trade-offs in applying fraudulent transfer law. Arguably, there are so many possible ways to divert value from creditors that it may be impossible to prohibit all possible fraudulent transfers

---

[13] 11 U.S.C. §544(b); 11 U.S.C. §548.

[14] 11 U.S.C.§548(a)(1)(A); UFTA §4(a)(1).

[15] UFTA §4(b).

[16] 11 U.S.C §548(2); UFTA §4(a)(2).

[17] 11 U.S.C. §548(c).

contractually. Some of these transactions, moreover, may be justifiable on efficiency grounds, making *ex ante* identification and prevention by the firm's affected creditors more difficult. These facts may justify *ex post* intervention to limit the costs of opportunism. But, as our model shows, expansive use of equitable remedies can give rise to opportunism by the parties it intends to protect. In this context, creditors (through bankruptcy trustees) have too much of an incentive to challenge non-opportunistic transactions as fraudulent. And the potential for judicial error in separating opportunistic from non-opportunistic transactions is high.

This criticism of fraudulent conveyance doctrine has been made most forcefully in the context of leveraged buyouts. In a typical leveraged buyout, the acquired firm takes on new secured debt to finance the purchase of the company's stock from its existing owners. The additional senior debt increases the default risk of the firm generally and decreases the value of the unsecured debt in place at the time of the transaction.

Because these transactions are challenged when a firm arrives in bankruptcy court, scholars such as Simkovic and Kaminetzky (2011) have noted the potential for hindsight bias in assessing the financial shakiness of the debtor at the time of the transaction. Other scholars such as Baird and Jackson (1985) also have noted that limits on future incurrence of secured debt can be, and often are, a common feature of contractual covenants in unsecured debt. Our comparative statics suggest that it may be sensible for equity to play a more limited role when there is high potential for judicial error, a large scope for opportunism on the part of the parties it intends to protect, or a greater ability for parties to protect themselves against opportunism contractually. This suggests that fraudulent transfer doctrine should play a more limited role in leveraged buyouts than it does under current law.

6 Discussion

Because formal legal rules generally cannot perfectly specify desirable conduct, they typically have areas of under-inclusion (loopholes), over-inclusion (snags), or both. The contracting examples and the patent example show that if one agent does not focus on the snags and loopholes, but evaluates conduct according to whether it is desirable, the other party may have a sufficient incentive to act desirably even in the shadow of the loopholes and snags.[18]

---

[18] This might suggest that the shadow of the law was actually doing some work among the ranchers described in Ellickson (1991). In that work, ranchers were able to cooperate despite the fact that the neighbors did not know what the law was and despite the fact that when they

We view the key feature of opportunism to be taking advantage of incompleteness of the law to an unusual or unexpected degree. In our model, garden-variety buyers lack the requisite knowledge to allow them to profitably exploit the incompleteness of the law, but there are other reasons why agents may not take full advantage of their formal legal rights. For one, many agents may internalize the broad intent of the law as fairness, or conversely, the law's intent may reflect what agents consider fair. These agents may have a distaste for misusing the law to achieve an unfair outcome.[19] Similarly, many agents are engaged in repeated interactions or are contracting in a context where they are affected by reputational concerns. These agents might suffer a cost to their reputation when they sue a supplier who provided a high-quality good. In fact, one might expect that these different features of garden-variety actors (concern for reputation, concern for fairness, and lack of knowledge of technicalities) are mutually reinforcing. If we defined garden-variety agents as agents who incur a psychic or reputational cost of c from suing when they receive a high-quality good, as opposed to opportunists, who are not constrained by concern for fairness or reputation, our results would be substantially identical.[20]

As long as there is enough correlation between the law and the desirable action, there can be an equilibrium where garden-variety, but self-interested, parties act as if they correspond exactly. Because acting desirably decreases the likelihood that the law is used, the law need not conform precisely with desirable behavior. However, the snags and loopholes become important when encountered by an opportunist, who is able to make strategic use of them. Because it is much easier to identify a particular use of a law as under- or over-inclusive *ex post*, this creates a rationale for equity, a flexible approach to the law.[21] However, the use of equity creates costs, particularly when there are doubts about the ability of the court to perfectly identify snags and loopholes. In fact, the attempt to discourage opportunism by one party can be used

---

were informed they found aspects of the law inefficient or unjust. This Element suggests that a belief that the law was approximately just, along with a lack of information about the details of the law, may have made it easier for them to sustain the cooperative equilibrium.

[19] For example, Feldman and Smith (2014) develop a distinction between compliance, where agents act in their own interest, but see the law as an external constraint, and opportunism, where agents take unintended and difficult-to-foresee advantage of the law. A key aspect of our argument, along with that of Feldman and Smith, is that agents and courts have a moral intuition that can *ex post* distinguish opportunistic use of the law.

[20] The only difference would be that these garden-variety types do not incur any cost from suing when the good is low quality; this would make the partial quality equilibrium more attractive relative to the low quality equilibrium.

[21] Equity as a correction of the law when it fails on account of its generality is a tradition that stretches back to Aristotle, who has often been invoked by judges and commentators (see Smith 2021, 156 and n.12, citing Aristotle, *The Nicomachean Ethics* 1137b, at 314–315, trans. H. Rackham, rev. ed., Cambridge, MA: Harvard University Press, 1934).

opportunistically by another party, and thus might be limited to cases where there is evidence of opportunism.

Our model captures important advantages of hybrid decision-making. These potential benefits can be found in many areas of the law, corresponding to both equitable and non-equitable devices. The equitable safety valve is not the only way to mix types of legal decision-making modes or even the only reason the law might combine rules and standards. The safety valve model does capture important aspects of the law, some of which have long resisted explanation or justification in economic terms. We now draw out some further implications.

6.1 Equity in Contracts

Equity has always been controversial and nowhere more so than in the area of contracts. Formalism and contextualism and *ex ante* versus *ex post* have always been central issues in contracts. With the advent of law and economics, the tendency of judges to hold parties' agreements up to standards ostensibly sounding in fairness and reasonableness has come in for heavy criticism. Why would judges be able to solve problems better than parties themselves? Once *ex ante* incentives are taken into account, aren't the *ex post* interventions of judges likely to make incentives worse rather than better? Law and economics scholars have brought the *ex ante* perspective back into the picture, making bright line rules tend to look better than they did at the height of realist-inspired contextualism (see, e.g., Bernstein 1996; Schwartz & Scott 2003). The contribution of law and economics has even led some to dub law and economics–inspired contract theory the "new formalism."

We return to the problems of opportunism and bounded rationality that form the heart of Williamson's approach to transaction cost economics. Williamson argued that the presence of opportunism implied the need for mostly *ex ante* devices in order to deter opportunism. That is, the *ex ante* mechanism would deter self-interest-seeking with guile.

Transaction cost economics recognizes a relationship between uncertainty (and bounded rationality) on the one hand and opportunism on the other. Uncertainty (also known as ambiguity) differs from risk in that the future event in question is not associated with a quantifiable probability, and radical uncertainty involves events that cannot be described at all (see, e.g., Knight 1921; Williamson 1985, 3–4, 56–59). (Or, in other words, risk involves known knowns and known unknowns, but uncertainty is further along the spectrum towards unknown unknowns.) Our model presented in Section 3 did not assume Knightian uncertainty (ambiguity), but we note here that a Williamsonian emphasis on behavioral uncertainty strengthens the case for equitable intervention. (It is also worth noting that a multiplicity of interacting possibilities of *ex post* actions and states of the world leads to complexity and *ex ante* intractability, which has much the same effect on behavior as uncertainty; MacLeod 2002.) In Williamson's framework, increased uncertainty leads to more opportunism, because the opportunist's performance cannot easily be measured. An opportunist can disguise the bad nature of their performance because it cannot be untangled from the other stochastic events, and this is particularly a problem *ex ante* when it is difficult to even describe such an event.

So, one way to reduce opportunism is to reduce uncertainty, hence the focus in transaction cost economics on *ex ante* devices, whether formal contracts or organizations: Performance can be more easily measured and so less shirking and deceit will occur. By leaving less scope for opportunism, *ex ante* devices make the contracting environment more certain. More generally, transaction cost economics sees opportunism as a problem of costly information. If information that could turn ambiguity into certainty, or at least into more measurable risk, is freely available, then there would be less loss from opportunism. The solutions proposed by transaction cost economics are designed to make information less costly and more available, and the major question is a comparative one: Which information-cost-lowering device is the most cost-effective? Nevertheless, nothing in principle rules out an *ex post* response to the problem of opportunism. Indeed, Williamson (1991, 273) hints at this when he mentions how excuse doctrine can be seen as a sparing response to injustice backed by "lawful" opportunism, while expressing the hope that it acts "ideally without adverse impact on incentives."

Our safety valve model of equity shows that the transaction cost approach needs to be generalized. Sometimes the most cost-effective device to deal with opportunism may involve *ex post* intervention, and it may require making information *more* costly to the opportunist. The problem as between an opportunist and a contracting partner, or between an opportunist and a court or other enforcer, is that the opportunist can exploit their information advantage. The opportunist has more information and can use it more effectively to wring unintended benefits out of the contract (or other law). But if the problem is relative information, then another possible avenue is to negate the opportunist's informational advantage, to keep them in the dark as to where they stand (up to a point). This is how equity fights fire with fire, as it were.

In a Williamsonian sense, equity is concerned with uncertainty that can be converted into risk (or certainty) by the opportunist. Uncertainty (ambiguity) gives rise to opportunism, because the opportunist can, for example, foresee how literalistic performance can have a very different value from what was foreseen. Even without the notion of uncertainty, opportunists have a lower cost of figuring out how to take unintended advantage of a contract (or other law) *ex post*. So on one reading of *Jacob & Youngs* v. *Kent*, 129 N.E. 889 (N.Y. 1921), the overriding danger is that the landowner is using a literal reading of the contract (insisting on Reading pipe rather than Reading-quality Cohoes pipe) in order to extort the builder. Garden-variety contracting parties have less ability to describe and to deal with unexpected events and so face genuine uncertainty. When an opportunist and a garden-variety person contract, the opportunist is effectively contracting over a different domain, to the detriment of the garden-variety person. The opportunist is playing on unforeseen or unintended dimensions. Thus, contractual incompleteness is pernicious because the contract is only one-sidedly incomplete. Knowing of this possibility in general, the garden-variety persons will be less willing to contract.

To counteract this possibility of differential bounded rationality in the face of uncertainty leading to opportunism, the Williamsonian transaction cost framework counsels the selection of a variety of *ex ante* institutions that lower the cost of information. In the area of contracts, default rules can sometimes deal with *ex post* opportunism. According to one view, the law uses *ex ante* information forcing default rules to present potential opportunists with a choice (see Ayres & Gertner 1989). Some parties with superior information might conceal it in order to contract in such a way that they get a larger payoff that is a larger piece of an overall smaller contractual pie. This is a form of opportunism. By setting the default against an informationally advantaged party, that party can either accept the default they don't want or contract around it, thereby revealing the information (and protecting the other party against the opportunism).

One particularly interesting *ex ante* device is to make the contract nominally complete, using a global information-forcing default rule. If we could be sure that one party is consistently better informed than the other on all issues, actual and potential, it can make sense to interpret the contract against that party. Any ambiguities would be resolved against the interest of that party. This makes the contract nominally complete, in that the ultimate default takes care of any remaining situations. And contract law does take this approach in limited circumstances. Thus, in insurance contracts the *contra proferentem* rule is applied against the insurer-drafter (see, e.g., Abraham 1996). A weaker version of this rule is applied against drafting parties (Restatement (Second) of Contracts §206 (1981); Ayres & Gertner 1989, 105 n.80), who have the opportunity to place hidden traps and are in a better position to control the language of a contract.

Information-forcing default rules are *ex ante*, like the other devices explored in traditional transaction cost economics, and they partake of the limitations of the *ex ante* approach. First of all, it is rare that one party is the potential opportunist across the board. Indeed, our model shows the dangers of either party exploiting the uncertainty of a contract. Once we have to distinguish potential opportunism issue by issue or situation by situation, then rule makers are vulnerable to getting it wrong and opening the door to opportunists.[22]

Our model suggests an extension of Williamson's scheme, to allow for *ex post* intervention that involves making information more costly – to the potential opportunist. The combination of opportunism and bounded rationality points to the possibility that the least-cost solution to the problem of opportunism will be *ex post* equitable intervention. Because of bounded rationality, contracting parties and lawmakers will find it impossible to keep up with all the potential dimensions of opportunism. Indeed, Williamson (1985, 58) notes that uncertainty of a strategic kind, which he terms behavioral uncertainty, has an inherent boundlessness, because "[t]he capacity for novelty in the human mind is rich beyond imagination." Deceit especially has this open-ended uncertainty, as the equity commentators realized. As Story put it, "[f]raud is infinite" given the "fertility of man's invention."[23] Williamson's approach resonates with the traditional concerns of equity, in which:

> The ingenuity of man in devising new forms of wrong cannot outstrip equity in its development. In all situations and under all circumstances, whether new or old, the principles of equity will point the way to justice where legal remedies are infirm. Precedents will be a constant guide, but never a bar. Where a new condition exists, and legal remedies afforded are inadequate or none are afforded at all, the never failing capacity of equity to adapt itself to all situations will be found equal to the case, extending old principles, if necessary, not adopting new ones, for that purpose.[24]

Or, as Chancellor Ellesmere put the point: "The Cause why there is a Chancery is, for that Mens Actions are so divers and infinite, That it is impossible to make any general Law which may aptly meet with every particular Act, and

---

[22] A possible example is the decision in *Campbell Soup Co.* v. *Wentz*, 172 F.2d 80 (3d Cir. 1948). In that case the court refused to grant specific performance to Campbell on the ground of unconscionability, but Goldberg (2006, 207–218) argues that the there was evidence that the Wentzes were acting opportunistically and that the insistence on specific performance was necessary for Campbell to prevent such opportunism by growers such as the Wentzes.

[23] Story (1836, §186, at 212) quoting a letter from Lord Hardwicke to Lord Kaims (June 30, 1759).

[24] *Harrigan* v. *Gilchrist*, 99 N.W. 909, 936 (Wis. 1904), quoted in Joseph Story, 1 Commentary on Equity Jurisprudence as Administered in England and America 4 (W. H. Lyon ed., 14th ed. 1918).

not fail in some Circumstances."[25] On this view, combating opportunism has to be at least in part judicial because of the open-endedness of opportunism. The ability of a better-informed party to engage in opportunism is hard to bound: Opportunism might occur on as yet unknown and undefined margins. It is not enough to say that contract law will supply defaults for incomplete contracts or that problems can be left to renegotiation. The problem is that widening the contractual domain (the state space it covers) might lead to the opposite from what one of the parties expected.

Although our model provides a reason to think that equity should be a strong default, these considerations of uncertainty point to how the model might be extended to provide a rationale for mandatory equity in some circumstances. For one thing, when asymmetric information is characterized as containing an element of uncertainty, we cannot expect contracting parties to anticipate it *ex ante* in any but the most general and unhelpful terms. To deal with the large discontinuities from exploited contractual uncertainty, contract law can benefit from some architectural ground rules and mileposts, including equity's anti-opportunism and the proxies on which it relies. Just as we don't allow parties to change the rules of contract formation and the rules of interpretation – although we allow them to specify within these ground rules the mode of acceptance and allow them to be their own lexicographer – there would be little to gain and much confusion to risk if we allowed people to contract out of equity altogether. And it is true that courts take a dim view of efforts to contract out of broad duties identified with anti-opportunism like the duty of good faith.[26] Specificity in a contract serves as evidence of the contract's domain and the contemplation of a particular problem, and under these circumstances the contract will displace equity.[27] Nevertheless, the safety valve is there in the legal infrastructure necessary to support exchange. Equity thus has a role even in an area of law as centered on party autonomy and intent as contracts.

An approach that incorporates equity stands in contrast to a strain of contract theory that eschews equity. In a series of articles, neo-formalist contract theorists have argued that equity is merely an unconstrained and misguided invocation of *ex post* fairness. Neo-formalists echo the common law lawyers of old in seeing equity as an *ex post* wild card, as a sanction motivated solely by fairness concerns, and an attempt to root out every last bit of hard-to-detect

---

[25] The Earl of Oxford's Case, 21 Eng. Rep. 485, 486 (Ch. 1615).

[26] Smith (2021, 1086–1087) discusses how good faith as a trigger for entering equity differs from more undefined and perhaps undefinable versions (contrast, e.g., Miller 2013; Kraus & Scott 2020).

[27] A specific statutory provision likewise displaces equity. See, for example, Indigo Realty Co. Charleston, 314 S.E.2d 601 (S.C. 1984); see also Young & Spitz 2003, 178–179.

opportunism (Kraus & Scott 2020; Scott 2015). Equity as "law about law" is more constrained and indeed orthogonal to many of these questions and builds on the idea that formalism and contextualism can be synergistic (Smith 2021).[28] Equity in contract law is not a loose employment of good faith nor is it an *ex post* wild card. A fortiori, our more limited focus here on equity as a safety valve for countering opportunism is not inconsistent with a substantial degree of formalism and does not require one to downplay party autonomy.

These debates about formalism in contract law often center on a small number of cases. Consider Schwartz and Scott's (2003, 615–616; 2008, 1614–1615, 1625–1629) take on *Jacob and Youngs* v. *Kent*, 129 N.E. 889 (N.Y. 1921). They see Judge Cardozo's opinion as sounding only in *ex post* waste and myopically getting in the way of what the contracting parties actually contracted for. Although the actual facts are a little obscure and have been endlessly discussed (see generally Goldberg 2015), the opinion is susceptible to an interpretation in which it is concerned with opportunism.[29] More specifically, the opinion's discussion of how idiosyncratic wishes have to be expressed is consistent with the idea that opportunists are operating outside of the domain of what was actually contracted about.[30] English law takes a similar approach, in which provisions that lead to strange and harsh results have to be expressed more clearly (even if this requires a "red hand" pointing to them).[31]

The problem here returns us to the issue of lack of intention, uncertainty, and intractability. Schwartz and Scott (2010, 948–951) are correct that strategic behavior is unlikely to be a large problem if formalist courts get the right answer under the contract more often than not. The problem arises where the opportunist can anticipate errors and can manipulate the opportunist's behavior so that the court's errors are not unbiased and the court can be expected (by the opportunist) to get it wrong more often than not.[32]

---

[28] Smith (2021) argues that it is consistent with a version of traditional equity to see it as operating over a defined domain and only coming into play with certain triggers based on various combinations of bad faith, undue hardship, and the like.

[29] Cohen (1992, 999–1000).

[30] Smith (2012, 909–991).

[31] *J. Spurling Ltd.* v. *Bradshaw* [1956] W.L.R. 461, 2 All E.R. 121 (Ct. App. 1956) (Denning, L.J.).

[32] A very similar issue arises in the choice between property rules and liability rules. A major argument for liability rules is that if courts get damages right on average, then actors have the correct internalizing incentives in expectation (see Kaplow & Shavell 1996). The court employs its best, unbiased estimate of situations taken from a fixed distribution (see Kaplow & Shavell 1996, 725–726, 776; see also Ayres & Goldbart 2001, 20–21, 23). But if a class of actors, whom we can call opportunists, knows enough about the proxies and actuarial classes a court will use, the opportunists can cherry-pick assets underpriced by liability rules; we cannot assume stable actuarial classes in the presence of opportunism. Smith (2004, 1774–1785; 2019, 57–59).

More generally, Kraus and Scott (2009) explicitly argue against traditional equity on the ground that it failed to distinguish contractual ends and contractual means and that equity wrongly assumed that parties' contracting over the former should be respected but not over the latter. They point out that the parties might, for their own value-maximizing reasons, care about and provide for the contractual means and not just the contractual ends. If so, *ex post* equitable intervention gets in the way of the parties' own deal and therefore reduces welfare. This argument holds but only over the domain over which the parties contract or, more accurately over the domain over which the parties can be expected to contract cost-effectively. Again, the difference between the garden-variety actor and an opportunist is that the latter is in effect playing on a larger field. Or to take another analogy, the opportunist is playing three-dimensional chess against a two-dimensional player.

Our safety valve model of equity also suggests an interpretation of the role of notice. To begin with, the concept of notice is crucial in many equitable doctrines. The basic reason is that someone is more likely to be an opportunist if they have notice of incompleteness of public or private law. The notion of bad faith in contract is also equitable and has an element of notice that can be seen as referring to the informational advantage that an opportunist is seeking to exploit. On the other hand, a party who has notice of a relevant fact is less likely to be the victim of opportunism. That party can more effectively self-protect. In particular, if someone has notice of a relevant fact *ex ante*, it is not uncertain. The contracting "domain" can be presumed to cover that fact.

6.2 Remedial Equity

The law faces a pervasive question whether the determination of liability should be a forgiving one or not and whether leniency should depend on the putative good faith of the actor. To take another example, under the doctrine of accession (Roman law specification), someone who mistakenly (in good faith) mixes labor with raw materials owned by another can keep the improved thing – say barrel hoops from raw timber or wine from grapes – if the improved thing is sufficiently transformed and/or more valuable than the raw material. But bad faith actors must simply return the improved good.

Equity as a safety valve against opportunism carries implications for remedies. As we have shown, the remedy against opportunists must be more severe than against garden-variety actors. One method of conforming to this requirement is to employ injunctions against suspected opportunists and also to withhold injunctive relief from opportunists. Those acting with unclean hands are not to be able to obtain an injunction, and leniency towards defendants – for example, by requiring a payment of damages but not subjecting them to injunctions – would not extend to those acting in bad faith (Chang 2015). The traditional standard also employed factors like "balancing of the equities," which means that equity might withhold an injunction where there is "disproportionate" or "undue" hardship.[33] "Balancing of the equities" thus does not mean hardships in equipoise, or cost-benefit analysis, but rather picks out situations in which an injunction would cause far greater harm to a (good-faith) defendant than it would bring benefit to the plaintiff, and this is a situation rife with dangers of opportunism by the plaintiff.[34] General concerns about unconscionability and anti-forfeiture principles important to recent mortgage crises can be understood as a core example of the equitable safety valve aimed at opportunistic parties, rather than necessarily being an unconstrained undoing of deals based solely on *ex post* fairness concerns. As we have seen, current issues with "patent trolls" are likewise a classic example of the value of the safety valve. Indeed, concerns about trolls have led the US Supreme Court and the federal judiciary into a strange and inadequate four-part test for injunctions (*eBay Inc.* v. *MercExchange, L.L.C.*, 547 U.S. 388, 391 (2006); Gergen et al. 2012), whereas the traditional safety valve approach can target the true opportunistic patent holders for special treatment.

However, as the controversies over patents trolls illustrate, equity as a safety valve is becoming harder to understand. After the merger of law and equity, the avowed boundaries of the equitable function – for example, as a safety valve – are harder to discern (Smith 2020). Phrases like "balance of the equities" are taken to mean true balancing of a quite unconstrained sort. The caricature of equity as unconstrained judicial discretion across the board threatens to come to life. Commentators have either embraced this problematic vision or have reacted against it with an extreme formalism. In the judicial realm, the polarization of positions on equity was on prominent display in *Grupo Mexicano de Desarrollo, S.A.* v. *Alliance Bond Fund, Inc.*, 527 U.S. 308 (1999), in which Justice Scalia read equity narrowly based on its scope in 1789 to hold that a federal court may not issue preliminary injunctions to freeze unrelated assets of a suspected opportunist in a suit in which only money damages were being sought. In dissent, Justice Ginsburg celebrated the flexibility and generativity of the equity power, with a mere nod to its limits. These polar positions of contextualism and formalism need not define

---

[33] Gergen et al. (2012).
[34] See Laycock (2012).

our views of equity, in light of the many hybrids available. That includes equity as a safety valve.[35]

6.3 Policy Implications and Empirical Predictions

As this Element has shown, equity is potentially compatible with a variety of theories of contract and a range of approaches to combining formalism and contextualism. The question is where, when, and how much to intervene in the operation of the law through equity. Substantive compliance is an equilibrium that requires protection. And in such situations, equity as a safety valve can serve as a hybrid decision-making mode suitable for dealing with a mixed population of garden-variety actors and opportunists.

Because our predictions about the effects and efficiency of the use of equity depend on the particular details of the transaction, it is difficult to derive many empirically testable implications. Indeed, in our model, the first order distributive effect of equity is to eliminate cross-subsidies, so the primary beneficiaries of are garden-variety buyers. If we were to alter our model so that sellers had some market power, we might find that extensive use of equity favors sellers in our model, but we could easily imagine a similar model in which opportunist sellers might be able to use a formal interpretation of a contract against a buyer. Thus, we don't generate predictions about whether or when equity is likely to generally favor buyers or sellers.

One might think that sellers could signal their lack of opportunism more easily than buyers. However, the very nature of the opportunism we study is that it takes a form that it is difficult for garden-variety actors to precisely anticipate, so it is not obvious how sellers could credibly directly signal that they are not opportunist. Another difficulty with signaling is that opportunists may have more to gain by convincing counterparties that they are garden-variety actors, because parties who discount the likelihood they are dealing with opportunists are more likely to leave themselves vulnerable. On the other hand, it is possible that sellers who deal with large numbers of buyers have more to lose by developing the reputation of being opportunists. To the degree that buyers are aware of these reputations, this does diminish the incentives for sellers to act opportunistically.[36]

It is not easy to generalize about the conditions under which it would be easier for courts to identify the various types of opportunists. However, Dari-Mattiacci and Guerriero (2015) suggest that the strength of society's culture of

---

[35] A sophisticated and somewhat more sympathetic reading of *Grupo Mexicano* and other recent "New Equity" cases in the US Supreme Court can be found in Bray (2015).

[36] See Friedman (2013) for an argument that this is less likely to occur in competitive markets.

Table 5 Equitable interventions

Less Complete Contracts		⇔		More Complete Contracts
Equitable Structures	Categorical Interventions	Remedies	Triggered Defenses	Triggered Interventions
Trusts, Corporations	Fiduciary Law, Confidential Relations, Misapproriations	Injunctions, Specific Performance, Constructive Trust	Clean Hands, Laches, Disproportionate Hardship	Unconscionability, Forfeiture

morality can affect the efficiency of various legal doctrines. To the degree that a society has a shared culture of morality, we might expect that this makes it easier for courts to identify opportunism that was not contemplated by one of the parties, and thus we might expect legal doctrine that permits more expansive use of equity.

Our findings suggest that as the incompleteness of contracts increases, there is more likely to be distance between substantive and technical compliance, and the desirability of equity increases. To the degree that rapid technological advancement, or legal or societal changes, entail a greater likelihood of unanticipated states, we would associate this with greater use of equity. This is consistent with the findings of Guerriero (2020), which reveal that in the presence of higher transaction costs property rights tend to be weaker.

As suggested by our simulation results, a court's willingness to use equity should depend on contextual matters, such as the degree of contractual imperfection, and the relatively likelihood of the various parties engaging opportunism. Table 5 shows a rough schematic of styles of equitable intervention in the middle row, with doctrines as examples in the bottom row. We group the interventions to illustrate that as we move from settings where there is less opportunity for complete contracts and specification, or settings where one party is clearly vulnerable to opportunism, to settings where more complete contracts are possible, or more likely to be symmetrical, use of equity tends to be more constrained and to require more evidence of bad faith or opportunism to trigger it.

7 Conclusion

Transaction cost economics counsels a comparative evaluation of devices to deal with opportunism in the face of bounded rationality. As developed by Oliver Williamson, this analysis involves mostly *ex ante* devices, flowing from contracts, organizations, or legal rules directly. The idea is to reduce the scope for opportunism by providing better information and thereby lowering uncertainty. In this Element, we have modeled how a decision-making mode with more than a passing resemblance to traditional equity can serve as a safety valve on the *ex ante* structures provided by the law when they can be manipulated in unintended ways. Strikingly, equity involves *ex post* intervention against such opportunism using proxies based on basic morality. Thus, what looks like myopic, unconstrained judicial meddling may instead be an effort to separate out the opportunists for harsher treatment. As long as the proxies used to identify the opportunists are good enough, some role for *ex post* equity can improve the efficiency of contracting. Even where contracting parties have the opportunity to address opportunism, equity polices the boundaries of their deal through doctrines based on notice. Far from equity's being discredited on economic grounds, our model points to the possibility of equitable intervention as a productive tool for countering opportunism, and our simulations suggest its continuing usefulness.

Appendix

A.1 Simulation

In order to make a meaningful comparative statics analysis, it is necessary to relax some of the simplifying assumptions we have made in earlier sections. In particular, to capture the negative welfare effects of the transfer from garden-variety buyers to opportunist buyers in a more continuous fashion, we want a model in which there is some elasticity in the market demand of both garden-variety and opportunist buyers.

A.1.1 Demand

To achieve elasticity of demand, we assume that potential buyers differ in their value for the good. Buyers, (indexed by k) get value $u_k + V$ from consuming the good, where u_k is the individual-specific value of a low-quality good and $V \in \{0, V_1\}$ is the value of quality described in Table 1, which is assumed to be constant across buyers. We assume that u_k is distributed with a constant density ϕ, and with a maximum value $\bar{u}$.[37] This implies that demand for the good will be linear in price, with slope ϕ. We also assume that the relative proportion of opportunist and garden-variety buyers (q and $1 - q$, respectively) is constant for all u_k.

The buyer's overall value of buying the good depends on their expected utility of consuming the good and the expected damages from lawsuits (which will depend on their type). In equilibrium, there will be some cutoff buyer types u^g_{min} and u^o_{min} that are indifferent between buying and not buying, so that all garden-variety buyers with $u_k \geq u^g_{min}$ and all opportunist buyers with $u_k \geq u^o_{min}$ purchase the good. For compactness, we use the symbol ψ_i to represent the likelihood that the court allows a plaintiff buyer to collect damages (i.e., the court denies the equitable defense for sellers) when the buyer is of type $i \in \{g, o\}$ and the court observes $y = 1$, but $a = 0$ (i.e., substantive, but not technical, compliance). This implies that $\psi_o = s(1 - \tau_o) + (1 - s)(1 - \tau_g)$ and $\psi_g = s(1 - \tau_g) + (1 - s)(1 - \tau_o)$. Optimal use of the signals requires that $\tau_o \geq \tau_g$, and $s > 0.5$, so it is straightforward to see that $\psi_g \geq \psi_o$.

A garden-variety buyer expects to get a quality good (through either substantive or technical compliance) from all non-opportunist sellers. When faced with an opportunist seller (with probability Ω), the garden-variety buyer

---

[37] Specifically, we assume that the maximum value for u_k is $\bar{u}$ and buyers are evenly distributed so that the mass of buyers with u_k in the interval $(u, \bar{u})$ is $\phi(\bar{u} - u)$ for any $u < \bar{u}$.

expects to receive a low-quality good and incur the cost c and sue, prevailing with probability ψ_g. Thus the net value the garden-variety buyer expects to receive from buying the good is:

$$(1 - \Omega)V_1 + \Omega(\psi_g D - c) + u_k - P.$$

This will sum to zero for a garden-variety buyer with $u_k = u^g_{min}$ who is indifferent between buying or not. Thus we can solve for the cutoff value

$$u^g_{min} = P - ((1 - \Omega)V_1 + \Omega(\psi_g D - c)).$$

Likewise, an opportunist buyer expects to receive a quality good (through either substantive or technical compliance) from all non-opportunist sellers. However, in addition to always suing opportunist sellers, the opportunist buyer will sue garden-variety sellers in the unusual state, because the seller will not be able to technically comply. Thus, the opportunist expects to sue with an additional probability $(1 - \Omega)\pi$. Furthermore, the opportunist buyer does not need to pay the cost c to sue. However, the court is more likely to apply equity against the opportunist buyer ($\psi_o < \psi_g$) so the net value they expect is:

$$(1 - \Omega)V_1 + (\Omega + (1 - \Omega)\pi)\psi_o D + u_k - P.$$

Solving for the cutoff value, we have:

$$u^o_{min} = P - ((1 - \Omega)V_1 + (\Omega + (1 - \Omega)\pi)\psi_o D).$$

With these assumptions in hand, total demand will be given by:

$$\phi((1 - q)(\bar{u} - u^g_{min}) + q(\bar{u} - u^o_{min})). \tag{A1}$$

We note that garden-variety (or opportunist) buyers whose value is u^g_{min} (or u^o_{min}) get no surplus from purchasing the good, whereas garden-variety (opportunist) buyers with the maximum value $\bar{u}$ receive surplus of $\bar{u} - u^g_{min}$ ($\bar{u} - u^o_{min}$). Given the uniform distribution of buyer types, the average welfare from a garden-variety (or opportunist) buyer is $\frac{\bar{u} - u^g_{min}}{2}$ (or $\frac{\bar{u} - u^o_{min}}{2}$). Thus total welfare for garden-variety (or opportunist) buyers is given by $\frac{(1-q)}{2}\phi(\bar{u} - u^g_{min})^2$ (or $\frac{q}{2}\phi(\bar{u} - u^o_{min})^2$). In this case, we use q^* to represent the actual equilibrium proportion of opportunists among all buyers. It is given by

$$q^* = \frac{q(\bar{u} - u^o_{min})}{(1 - q)(\bar{u} - u^g_{min}) + q(\bar{u} - u^o_{min})}.$$

A.2 Supply

We assume that there is an infinite supply of honest sellers with cost z_L as before, but here we add some elasticity in the decision to enter by opportunist sellers. Thus, it may no longer be optimal (or practical) to keep all opportunist sellers out of the market, but it is still desirable to minimize their presence. Specifically, we assume there is a continuum of mass θ of opportunist sellers indexed by j with cost z_j, where z_j is uniformly distributed over the interval $[z_O, z_L]$. Thus, the quantity that enter will be linear in their expected revenue from entering. Since an opportunist seller does not provide a quality good but does expect to get sued, their additional cost of providing the good will be the expected damages they will pay. A proportion q^* of their customers will be opportunist buyers who will prevail with probability ψ_o, while the remaining $(1 - q^*)$ are garden-variety and prevail with probability ψ_g. Thus, expected damages are

$$D((1 - q^*)\psi_g + q^*\psi_o)$$

and their net profit from entering would be $P - D((1 - q^*)\psi_g + q^*\psi_o) - z_j$. Thus, any opportunists with cost less than $z_{max} = P - D((1 - q^*)\psi_g + q^*\psi_o)$ will enter, so the mass of opportunist sellers who enter will be

$$\theta \frac{z_{max} - z_O}{z_L - z_O} = \frac{\theta(P - D((1 - q^*)\psi_g + q^*\psi_o) - z_O)}{z_L - z_O}. \tag{A2}$$

A.2.1 Equilibrium and Total Welfare

In equilibrium, the number of sellers must equal the number of buyers. The total number of buyers is given in equation (A1), and the number of opportunist sellers is given by (A2). In equilibrium, the garden-variety sellers will supply the remainder of the demanded goods. Therefore, the proportion of opportunist sellers in equilibrium is given by

$$\Omega = \frac{\theta(z_{max} - z_O)}{(z_L - z_O)\phi((1 - q)(\bar{u} - u^g_{min}) + q(\bar{u} - u^o_{min}))}.$$

Note that the honest sellers are held to zero profit in equilibrium, so total welfare is the sum of the surplus of the garden-variety buyers, the opportunist buyers, and the opportunist sellers. From above, the average welfare for a garden-variety purchaser or an opportunist purchaser is given by $\frac{\bar{u} - u^g_{min}}{2}$ or $\frac{\bar{u} - u^o_{min}}{2}$ respectively. Similarly, if z_{max} is the cost to the highest cost opportunist seller who enters, the average welfare for an opportunist seller is $\frac{z_{max} - z_O}{2}$, so the total welfare to opportunist sellers is $\frac{\theta(P - D((1-q^*)\psi_g - -q^*\psi_o) - z_O)^2}{2(z_L - z_O)}$.

Honest sellers are held to zero profits, so total welfare is given by:

$$W = \frac{\phi}{2}((1 - q)(\bar{u} - u^g_{min})^2 + q(\bar{u} - u^o_{min})^2)$$
$$+ \frac{\theta(P - D((1 - q^*)\psi_g - -q^*\psi_o) - z_O)^2}{2(z_L - z_O)}.$$

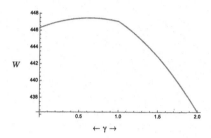

Figure A1 Total welfare vs. γ ($\theta = 0.4$)

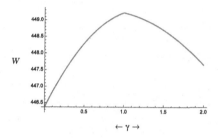

Figure A2 Total welfare vs. γ ($\theta = 0.07$)

In a substantive compliance equilibrium, the following conditions are all satisfied: an honest seller provides high quality in both states (IC); honest sellers make zero profit (ZP) so the market clears; and the proportion of opportunist sellers (OS), garden-variety buyers (GV), and opportunist buyers (OB) is consistent with beliefs in equilibrium.

We assign default values as follows:

$$\phi = 1, \theta = 0.25, s = 0.7, z_L = 20, z_O = -30, V = 50,$$
$$\pi = 0.15, q = 0.2, \bar{u} = 0, z_{max} = 50.$$

We use the Mathematica (Wolfram) software program to identify the value of γ that maximizes welfare. Plots of welfare as a function of γ suggest that it is well-behaved and concave for $\gamma \in (0, 1)$ and has a kink downward at $\gamma = 1$, where $\tau_o = 1$, and any further increase in equity must be applied against garden-variety buyers (see Figures A1 and A2, which plot total welfare against γ).

We also note that opportunist buyer welfare is decreasing in extent of equity (γ), while opportunist seller welfare is increasing. When $\gamma < 1$, garden-variety buyer's welfare tends to be increasing due to the decrease in cross-subsidy (unless θ is high and γ is high already, in which case it might decrease due to entry by opportunist sellers). As long as $s > 0.5$, there is a kink downwards in garden-variety buyers' welfare and a kink upwards in opportunist buyers' welfare. See Figures A3, A4, and A5.

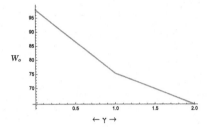

Figure A3 Opportunist buyers' welfare vs. γ ($\theta = 0.4$)

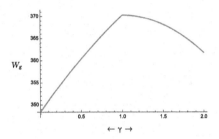

Figure A4 Garden-variety buyers' welfare vs. γ ($\theta = 0.4$)

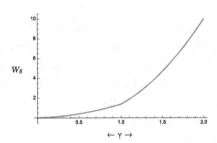

Figure A5 Opportunist sellers' welfare vs. γ ($\theta = 0.4$)

A.3 Optimal Equity

Setting an optimal level of equity consists of finding a point where the marginal benefit of decreasing the transfer from garden-variety to opportunist buyers is balanced by the marginal harm from decreasing the deterrence of opportunist sellers. Our simulation operates by assigning values to the parameters of the model and numerically finding the degree of equity that maximizes welfare. We take advantage of the fact that it is always optimal to increase τ_o to the maximum value and always apply equity when the buyer appears to be opportunist before increasing τ_g above 0 and ever applying equity to buyers who appear to be garden-variety. We define $\gamma \in [0, 2]$ as the sum of $\tau_o + \tau_g$ and note that $\tau_o = \min(\gamma, 1)$ and $\tau_g = \max(0, 1 - \gamma)$. The simulation then identifies the value of γ that maximizes welfare. The plots in the body of the Element (Figures 1–5) show how the corresponding values of τ_o and τ_g vary with the parameters.

References

Abraham, Kenneth S. 1996. "A Theory of Insurance Policy Interpretation," 95 *Michigan Law Review* 531–569.

Aghion, Philippe & Benjamin Hermalin. 1990. "Legal Restrictions on Private Contracts Can Enhance Efficiency," 6 *Journal of Law, Economics, and Organization* 381–409.

Allison, John, Mark A, Lemley, & David L. Schwartz. 2017. "How Often Do Non-practicing Entities Win Patent Suits?" 32 *Berkeley Technology Law Journal* 235–308.

Ayres, Ian & Robert Gertner. 1989. "Filling Gaps in Incomplete Contracts: An Economic Theory of Default Rules," 99 *Yale Law Journal* 87–130.

Ayres, Ian & Paul M. Goldbart. 2001. "Optimal Delegation and Decoupling in the Design of Liability Rules," 100 *Michigan Law Review* 1–79.

Baird, Douglas G. & Thomas H. Jackson. 1985. "Fraudulent Conveyance Law and Its Proper Domain," 38 *Vanderbilt Law Review* 829–855.

Bar-Gill, Oren & Omri Ben-Shahar. 2009. "An Information Theory of Willful Breach," 107 *Michigan Law Review* 1479–1499.

Bernstein, Lisa. 1996. "Merchant Law in a Merchant Court: Rethinking the Code's Search for Immanent Business Norms," 144 *University of Pennsylvania Law Review* 1765–1821.

Bray, Samuel. 2015. "The Supreme Court and the New Equity," 68 *Vanderbilt Law Review* 997–1054.

Chang, Yun Chien. 2015. "An Economic and Comparative Analysis of *Specificatio* (the Accession Doctrine)," 39 *European Journal of Law and Economics* 225–243.

Choi, Albert & George Triantis. 2008. "Completing Contracts in the Shadow of Costly Verification," 37 *Journal of Legal Studies* 503–534.

Choi, Albert & George Triantis. 2010. "Strategic Vagueness in Contract Design: The Case of Corporate Acquisitions," 119 *Yale Law Journal* 848–924.

Cohen, George M. 1992. "The Negligence-Opportunism Tradeoff in Contract Law," 20 *Hofstra Law Review* 941–1016.

Cohen, George M. 2009. "The Fault That Lies within Our Contract Law," 107 *Michigan Law Review* 1445–1460.

Craswell, Richard. 2009. "When Is a Willful Breach 'Willful'? The Link between Definitions and Damages," 107 *Michigan Law Review* 1501–1515.

Dari-Mattiacci, Guiseppe & Carmine Guerriero. 2015. "Law and Culture: A Theory of Comparative Variation in Bona Fide Purchase Rules," 35 *Oxford Journal of Legal Studies* 543–574.

Ehrlich, Isaac & Richard Posner. 1974. "An Economic Analysis of Legal Rulemaking", 3 *The Journal of Legal Studies* 257–286.

Ellickson, Robert C. 1991. *Order without Law: How Neighbors Settle Disputes.* Cambridge, MA: Harvard University Press.

Epstein, Richard A. 1975. "Unconscionability: A Critical Reappraisal," 18 *Journal of Law & Economics* 293–315.

Feldman, Yuval & Henry E. Smith. 2014. "Behavioral Equity," 170 *Journal of Institutional and Theoretical Economics* 137–159.

Friedman, Ezra. 2013. "Competition and Unconscionability," 15 *American Law and Economics Review* 443–494.

Friedman, Ezra & Abraham Wickelgren. 2014. "A New Angle on Rules versus Standards," 16 *American Law and Economics Review* 499–549.

Friedmann, Daniel. 1989. "The Efficient Breach Fallacy," 18 *Journal of Legal Studies* 1–24.

Ganglmair, Bernhard. 2017. "Efficient Material Breach of Contract," 33 *Journal of The Journal of Law, Economics, and Organization* 507–540.

Gergen, Mark P., John M. Golden, & Henry E. Smith. 2012. "The Supreme Court's Accidental Revolution? The Test for Permanent Injunctions," 112 *Columbia Law Review* 203–249.

Goldberg, Victor P. 1989. *Readings in the Economics of Contract Law.* Cambridge: Cambridge University Press.

Goldberg, Victor P. 2006. *Framing Contract Law: An Economic Perspective.* Cambridge, MA: Harvard University Press.

Goldberg, Victor P. 2015. "Rethinking *Jacob & Youngs* v. *Kent*," 66 *Case Western Reserve Law Review* 111–142.

Gordley, James. 1981. "Equality in Exchange," 69 *California Law Review* 1587–1656.

Guerriero, Carmine. 2020 "Property Rights, Transaction Costs, and the Limits of the Market". Quaderni – Working Paper DSE N° 1110.

Kaplow, Louis. 1992. "Rules versus Standards," 42 *Duke Law Journal* 557–629.

Kaplow, Louis & Steven Shavell. 1996. "Property Rules versus Liability Rules: An Economic Analysis," 109 *Harvard Law Review* 713–790.

Kaplow, Louis & Steven Shavell. 2002. *Fairness versus Welfare.* Cambridge, MA: Harvard University Press.

Knight, Frank H. 1921. *Risk, Uncertainty, and Profit.* Boston, MA: Houghton Mifflin Company.

Kostristsky, Juliet P. 2007. "Plain Meaning vs. Broad Interpretation: How the Risk of Opportunism Defeats a Unitary Default Rule for Interpretation," 96 *Kentucky Law Journal* 43–98.

Kraus, Jody & Robert E. Scott. 2009. "Contract Design and the Structure of Contractual Intent," 84 *New York University Law Review* 1023–1104.

Kraus, Jody P. & Robert E. Scott. 2020. "The Case Against Equity in American Contract Law," 93 *University of Southern California Law Review* 1323–1383.

Kronman, Anthony T. 1978. "Mistake, Information, and the Law of Contracts," 7 *Journal of Legal Studies* 1–34.

Laycock, Douglas. 2012. "The Neglected Defense of Undue Hardship (and the Doctrinal Train Wreck in *Boomer* v. *Atlantic Cement*)" 4 *Journal of Tort Law* Article 3. 10.1515/1932-9148.1123, https://www.degruyter.com/journal/key/jtl/4/3/html.

MacLeod, W. Bentley. 2002. "Complexity and Contract," in Eric Brousseau & Jean-Michel Glachant, eds., *The Economics of Contracts: Theories and Applications* 213–240. Cambridge: Cambridge University Press.

Masten, Scott. 1988. "Equity, Opportunism and the Design of Contractual Relations," 144 *Journal of Institutional and Theoretical Economics* 180–195.

Miller, Alan D. & Ronen Perry. 2013. "Good Faith Performance," 98 *Iowa Law Review* 689–745.

Muris, Timothy. 1981. "Opportunistic Behavior and the Law of Contracts," 65 *Minnesota Law Review* 521–590.

Rose, Carol M. 1988. "Crystals and Mud in Property Law," 40 *Stanford Law Review* 577–610.

Schwartz, Alan & Robert E. Scott. 2003. "Contract Theory and the Limits of Contract Law," 113 *Yale Law Journal* 541–619.

Schwartz, Alan & Robert E. Scott. 2008. "Market Damages, Efficient Contracting, and the Economic Waste Fallacy," 108 *Columbia Law Review* 1610–1669.

Schwartz, Alan & Robert E. Scott. 2010. "Contract Interpretation Redux," 119 *Yale Law Journal* 926–964.

Scott, Robert & George Triantis. 2006. "Anticipating Litigation in Contract Design," 115 *Yale Law Journal*, 814–879.

Scott, Robert E. 2009. "In (Partial) Defense of Strict Liability in Contract," 107 *Michigan Law Review* 1381–1396.

Scott, Robert E. 2015. "Contract Design and the Shading Problem," 99 *Marquette Law Review* 1–28.

Shavell, Steven. 2009. "Why Breach of Contract May Not Be Immoral Given the Incompleteness of Contracts," 107 *Michigan Law Review* 1569–1581.

Shiffrin, Seana Valentine. 2007. "The Divergence of Contract and Promise," 120 *Harvard Law Review* 708–753.

Simkovic, Michael & Benjamin S. Kaminetzky. 2011. "Leveraged Buyout Bankruptcies, The Problem of Hindsight Bias, and the Credit Default Swap Solution." 1 *Columbia Business Law Review* 118–257.

Smith, Henry E. 2004. "Property and Property Rules," 79 *New York University Law Review* 1719–1798.

Smith, Henry E. 2011. "Rose's Human Nature of Property," 19 *William and Mary Bill of Rights Journal* 1047–1055.

Smith, Henry E. 2012. "The Equitable Dimension of Contract," 45 *Suffolk University Law Review* 897–914.

Smith, Henry E. 2017. "Fusing the Equitable Function in Private Law," in Kit Barker, Karen Fairweather, & Ross Grantham, eds., *Private Law in the 21st Century* 173–195. Oxford: Hart Publishing.

Smith, Henry E. 2019. "Complexity and the Cathedral: Making Law and Economics More Calabresian," 48 *European Journal of Law and Economics* 43–63.

Smith, Henry E. 2020. "Fusion of Law and Confusion of Equity," in Dennis Klimchuk, Irit Samet, & Henry E. Smith, eds., *Philosophical Foundations of the Law of Equity* 210–230. Oxford: Oxford University Press.

Smith, Henry E. 2021. "Equity as Meta-Law," 130 *Yale Law Journal* 1050–1144. (Earlier versions include: Smith Henry E. 2015, "Equity as Second-Order Law: The Problem of Opportunism" (January 15, 2015), http://ssrn.com/abstract=2617413(https://perma.cc/JQ3G-8Z3M) and Smith, Henry E. ms. "An Economic Analysis of Law versus Equity," https://law.yale.edu/sites/default/files/area/workshop/leo/document/HSmith_LawVersusEquity7.pdf).

Spier, Kathryn E. 1992. "Incomplete Contracts and Signalling," 23 *The RAND Journal of Economics*, 432–443.

Story, Joseph. 1836. *Commentaries on Equity Jurisprudence: As Administered in England and America.* Boston, MA: Hilliard, Gray & Co.

Stremitzer, Alexander. 2012. "Opportunistic Termination," 28 *Journal of Law, Economics, and Organization* 381–406.

Williamson, Oliver E. 1985. *The Economic Institutions of Capitalism: Firms, Markets, Relational Contracting.* New York: Free Press.

Williamson, Oliver E. 1991. "Cooperative Economic Organization: The Analysis of Discrete Structural Alternatives," 36 *Administrative Science Quarterly* 269–296.

Williamson, Oliver E. 1993. "Opportunism and Its Critics," 14 *Managerial and Decision Economics* 97–107.

Young, Roger & Stephen Spitz. 2003. "SUEM – Spitzs; Ultimate Equitable Maxim: In Equity, Good Guys Should Win and Bad Guys Should Lose," 55 *South Carolina Law Review* 175–189.

Acknowledgment

For helpful comments, the authors thank Gillian Hadfield, Scott Baker, Giuseppe Dari-Mattiaci, and participants at the 2012 Haas/Sloan Conference on Law, Economics & Organization, the 2012 Theoretical Law and Economics Conference at Yale, and the UCLA Law and Economics Workshop. We are also indebted to three anonymous referees.

Cambridge Elements ≡

Law, Economics and Politics

Series Editor in Chief

Carmine Guerriero, *University of Bologna*

Series Co-Editors

Alessandro Riboni, *École Polytechnique*
Jillian Grennan, *Duke University, Fuqua School of Business*
Petros Sekeris, *Montpellier Business School*

Series Managing Editor

Valentino Moscariello, *University of Bologna*

Series Associate Editors

Maija Halonen-Akatwijuka, *University of Bristol*
Sara Biancini, *Université de Cergy-Pontoise*
Melanie Meng Xue, *London School of Economics and Political Science*
Claire Lim, *Queen Mary University of London*
Andy Hanssen, *Clemson University*
Giacomo Benati, *Eberhard Karls University, Tübingen*

About the Series

Decisions taken by individuals are influenced by formal and informal institutions. Legal and political institutions determine the nature, scope and operation of markets, organisations, and states. This interdisciplinary series analyses the functioning, determinants, and impact of these institutions, organizing the existing knowledge and guiding future research.

Cambridge Elements ☰

Law, Economics and Politics

Elements in the Series

The Strategic Analysis of Judicial Behavior: A Comparative Perspective
Lee Epstein and Keren Weinshall

Can Blockchain Solve the Hold-up Problem in Contracts?
Richard Holden and Anup Malani

Deep IV in Law: Appellate Decisions and Texts Impact Sentencing in Trial Courts
Zhe Huang, Xinyue Zhang, Ruofan Wang and Daniel L. Chen

Reform for Sale
Perrin Lefebvre and David Martimort

A Safety Valve Model of Equity as Anti-opportunism
Kenneth Ayotte, Ezra Friedman and Henry E. Smith

A full series listing is available at: www.cambridge.org/ELEP

Printed in the United States
by Baker & Taylor Publisher Services